Sell a Children's Book NOW!

QUICK SUCCESS

IN THE

EDUCATIONAL MARKET

Mike Downs and Sandra K. Athans

Your Educational Dream Team

To Our Readers

We dedicate this book to YOU, and to all of our hard-working, passionate, educational writer friends, editors, publishers, workshop attendees, interested followers, and other kidlit colleagues, who share this exhilarating adventure that is the Educational Marketplace!

Special Thanks

We are especially grateful to the writers who contributed samples and suggestions to bolster the authentic experience for our readers. You'll find their wonderful contributions in the appendix.

Finally, we are thankful for the young readers who keep us energized as they learn and grow through reading. We look forward to hearing about the many wondrous new children's books that will appear as the result of this book!

Sandra & Mike

*Enter here to discover
the wonderfully fulfilling, furiously paced, research
laden, playfully fun, demandingly strict BUT incredibly
rewarding world of Educational Publishing.*

Mike Downs and Sandra K. Athans

Come on in!

If you're searching for a comprehensive, fun-to-read, easy-to-understand book about the *Educational Market*, you're in the right place.

In earlier searches you may have uncovered snippets of Educational Publishing. Perhaps you even sifted through enough books and web pages to glean a few nuggets of tantalizing need-to-know information about this complex publishing marketplace. But where, you wondered, was that easy-to-read, clearly understandable resource that provided the exact information necessary for you to successfully break into the market.

You found it!

Sell a Children's Book NOW - Quick Success in the Educational Market, details the inner workings of this confusing market and clearly explains its many parts. But that's not all! It also includes a spectacular gem sparkling inside—A STEP-BY-STEP GUIDE that sets you on a path to getting a book contract in the Educational Market *fast*—often in less than six months.

WOW!

Did we say *less than six months?* That is absolutely right! These proven steps have taken dozens of authors from zero knowledge of the market to *signing contracts* for one or more books in a series, in *less than six months.* Incredible!

How is that possible?

The trick is having a clear understanding of this perplexing market and a *step-by-step plan* on how to approach it. Unlike the glacially slow-paced *Trade Market,* the *Educational Market* moves at breakneck speed. This means you could possibly be holding your very own, traditionally published photo-illustrated-picture-book in your hand in less than a year. In fact, we've had books *published* within six months of our *initial manuscript submission.*

The type of book noted above, a photo-illustrated-picture-book, is a large segment of the *Educational Market.* These books cover a huge array of topics, primarily in the nonfiction category. The topics are chosen by the publisher and assigned by an editor. As an author, if you agree to write one, you'll carefully research and quickly write the manuscript. Writers who tackle these titles are comfortable doing concise and accurate research. If that sounds like you, or could sound like you with some guidance, then you'll be thrilled! Most new writers break into the *Educational Market* by writing this type of photo-illustrated, nonfiction manuscript.

However, nonfiction photo-illustrated-picture-books are only a part of the story. Fiction, poetry, and memoirs are also a part of this market—they're simply less likely to be landed as a first assignment. There are also lots of other exciting opportunities that you'll rarely discover outside this book. These include creating test passages, writing teacher instructional guides, developing student study guides, writing skits, readers' theater and more. The *Educational Market* is filled with opportunity!

And there's another more profound aspect of this industry. The *Educational Market* reaches directly into schools and other educational settings. This means your published materials will line the shelves of school libraries and teacher resource collections. Your books will be enjoyed by kids sprawled on the carpeted floors of library reading areas as they read for enjoyment or learn to grasp tricky concepts. Teachers will use your work to strengthen and spice up lessons.

In this market, your writing can expand a child's view of the world and steer them toward a lifelong love of reading.

How cool is that!

Sell a Children's Book NOW - Quick Success in the Educational Market, will set you up for a trifecta of successes. You can earn some money, fulfill your dream of having your very own book published, and make a positive impact on the lives of young readers. You might even end up with your own series! In this burgeoning and vibrant market there's plenty of room for everyone.

So come on in. Take the plunge. All you have to do is turn the page.

We'll see you inside.

ABOUT THE AUTHORS

We know what you're thinking. Who could put together a book that covers the widely varied, multi-tentacled opportunities of educational publishing, *and,* explain it in a simple, straight-forward manner? That's a lot of ground to cover!

You are absolutely right.

That's why we *co-authored* this book. Yep. Two authors. We wanted the information to be comprehensive, current, insightful, and fun. We wanted you to know about *every* opportunity you have to publish your first picture book or create teacher related materials in this specialized market. Mike is especially up-to-date on the carefully researched *nonfiction-photo-picture-book* segment of the market. He has also sold *poetry, fantasy,* and *memoir* picture books. If these interest you, Mike will provide the guidance you need for success.

We also wanted to highlight *other segments* of educational publishing that are typically neglected. A multitude of additional opportunities are available, *especially* to those with a background in education. This is where Sandra's knowledge and experience shine. To name just a few lesser known opportunities, there are *reader's theater skits, lesson plans, teacher's guides, and test passages.* Sandra will steer you to success in all of these categories.

So what are you waiting for? Teachers, counselors, coaches, aides, involved parents, and all other educators... come on in for *double the opportunity!*

With that said, we'd like to introduce you to our team. First up is Mike Downs.

Mike Downs

Before I began writing in the Educational Market, I already had a couple Trade Market picture books in stores. But those had been written nearly 15 years earlier. I had given up writing for many years and wasn't having any luck trying to reenter the market in 2018. I was also *totally* clueless about the *Educational Market*. Then, in the summer of 2018, a confluence of fortunate events sent me careening toward this new opportunity. I had upcoming vacation time, I noticed a Highlights Workshop on the *Educational Market,* and I had just enough money stashed away to attend it. I hoped that learning about this different market would be a great opportunity to improve my writing skills. Maybe even sell some books. This proved to be absolutely true! It was at Highlights where I met my future co-author, Sandra K. Athans, one of the workshop facilitators. But back to me.

The workshop was amazing. Over the course of four days a lot of writers, including me, learned the tools of the trade that would gain us entry into educational publishing. However, when I finished the workshop and searched for other information on educational writing, all I found was a disjointed array of articles and a single book. None provided the clear blueprint I was looking for.

Seeing this hole in the marketplace, I knew I would eventually be interested in writing that book myself. A book that would give a clear understanding of the educational publishing industry while setting new writers on the shortest path to meeting their own writing goals and dreams.

First, I had a lot of work to do.

In the next three years, I pitched publishers, researched books, and wrote...and wrote... and wrote. In those three years I sold thirteen *nonfiction-photo-picture-books*. They were carefully researched books about aviation, continents, outer space, and even gluten (that book is a story in itself!). I sold an additional seven books in the *poetry, fantasy,* and *memoir* categories. These latter books are notoriously difficult to sell in the *Educational Market.* The books sold to major publishers such as ABDO, Rourke Educational, and Heinemann.

Through trial—and plenty of error—I figured out how to target educational publishers and give them exactly what they wanted. That's what we'll explain in this book. That's what *you'll* soon be doing.

But I was left with a problem. I could only speak authoritatively about the type of books that *I* had sold. That was great! But I was unfamiliar with a huge segment of the market—those projects written specifically for the educational system. That's where Sandra comes in. Not only has she sold nonfiction-photo-picture-books, she has also sold a wide variety of other educational related materials at both the picture book and adult levels. So, now is a good time to leave me behind and let Sandra share her story.

Sandra K. Athans

Unlike Mike, I didn't stumble into opportunity. Instead, I made my own—which is what I like to do. That's likely the same gusto and spirit that prompted you to pick up this book!

If you have a background—or a passion—in education, you'll be thrilled to learn that educational publishers will welcome you...and quite likely grow to *adore you!* How's that for a joyful invitation to the market? We'll help you get there!

I was 40 years old when I began my second career as a teacher and budding writer. I entered the field of educational writing because I was passionate about helping kids learn to read and write. That, together with my own love for reading and writing, set the stage for my *backdoor* entry into the educational publishing industry.

As a new teacher, I was eager to find great books I could use for teaching. In my search, I discovered there were literacy conferences which offered sessions for professional growth, and—huge bonus here—where hundreds of publishers exhibited their products! I spent hours perusing their books, often thinking *I could write this* or sometimes even, *I could write this...better!*

My new teaching experience gave me an edge for gauging what would work with students. I could pin-point gaps in the market—things that weren't yet available...but should be.

With these insights, I began contacting publishers directly to ask for work and sometimes to pitch original ideas.

Much later I learned there was an easier process for entering this market. One where you didn't need to attend literacy conferences or approach publishing bigwigs face-to-face. Darn it! How did I miss that information? I'll save my techniques for the *claw-your-way-in-the-backdoor* approach for my next book!

For the next fifteen years I was fortunate to get an ever-increasing volume of work with top-notch publishers like Scholastic, Pearson, Rosen, Corwin, Millbrook, Carus, and Rourke Educational. I worked on hundreds of projects: a seven-volume *series on school standards,* countless *lesson plans, teachers' guides* (including a 100 book volume of ebooks), *project templates* for literacy collections, *reader's theater skits, nonfiction books* and *early readers.* I also wrote for kid's magazines and co-authored *five teacher resource books* on reading and writing.

And YES—before you ask—the answer is *you can do this, too!* Time, effort, and the knowledge you get from this book will give you a head-start in achieving your own successes. If you put in the work, the results will follow.

Before I close out this section, I'd like to circle back to emphasize a couple of items.

First, I should note that Mike failed to mention a very important point—we both did all of our writing while working full time. If you prioritize time for yourself, you can do the same.

Second, I'd like to reiterate that you'll have the opportunity to work closely with an editor as you complete each manuscript. With your educational savvy, you'll get to talk shop with your contacts, build rich relationships, and even influence their decisions. Mingling in the Educational Market in these ways is rewarding and adds a unique dimension of fun to the hard work you'll be undertaking!

Now have at it, enjoy the journey, and turn the page.

TABLE OF CONTENTS

Chapter 1 *PAGE 1*

Educational Market vs. Trade Market

2   Queries
3   The Manuscript
4   Pay and Royalties
4   Speed to Publication
5   Marketing

Chapter 2 *PAGE 7*

Why You Should Write for the Educational Market

7   You Can Change the World
8   Fortune and Fame
9   Improve Writing Skills

Chapter 3 *PAGE 11*

Which Educational Market Publisher Fits You?

11   The Heart and Soul
      of Publishers
13   What's Their Angle?
15   Finding Your Publishers
16   Get a List of Educational
      Publishers
17   Read Their Books
17   Keep a List of What You Like

Chapter 4 *PAGE 18*

Writing Opportunities

18   Opportunities
19   Nonfiction
19   Fiction
20   Teacher Related Products
20   What Reading Level Will You
      Write For?
22   Don't Hold Out for the
      Perfect Project

Chapter 5   *PAGE 23*

Your Submission Package

24   The Query Letter
27   Your Resume
30   Writing Samples
32   Unedited Writing Samples
32   Publisher Specified Samples
33   Word Count
34   What Editors Look For
36   Lesson Plans
37   A Final Word on Samples

Chapter 6   *PAGE 39*

Step-by-Step Guide to Success— Enter the Educational Market in only 8 Weeks!

Chapter 7   *PAGE 43*

Landing Assignments

44   You Did It!
44   Project Offer Attachments
46   Reviewing Your Documents
46   Author Guidelines
49   The Contract
51   Manuscript Template
52   Ready. Set. Go!

Chapter 8   *PAGE 54*

Research. Research. Research.

55   Researching Your Topic
58   Using Experts

Chapter 9   *PAGE 60*

Writing Your Manuscript

61   The Manuscript Outline
62   On to the Story
62   ATOS, Lexile, and Leveling
64   Sneaky Sidebars
68   Tempting Titles
68   Hook and Tone
69   Document Everything Now
72   Accuracy is the Key to Success
74   Sensitive Content
77   Trite and Overused
78   Art Specs. Photographs. Visuals
79   Glossary
80   Index
80   Curious Questions
81   Extension Activities
82   Author Bio and Picture
83   Chat GPT and AI
85   Academic Standards

Chapter 10   *PAGE 88*

Deadlines and Submissions

88 Deadlines
90 Manuscript Outline
91 Manuscript Formatted and
      Complete
92 Proof Copies

Chapter 11   *PAGE 93*

What's Next

93 Invoice
94 Author's Copies
94 Taxes
94 Job Cycles
97 Academia and Lessons
98 Staying Connected
102 Editors That Move
103 Spreading Your Wings to the
      Trade Market
104 Pitching a Series

Chapter 12   *PAGE 106*

Onward!

Attachments

110 Queries
120 Writing Samples
137 Resumes
143 Interview Requests
148 FAQ (Dueling FAQ's by
       Sandra and Mike)

Sell a Children's Book NOW:
Quick Success in the Educational Market

CHAPTER 1

Educational Market vs Trade Market

What the heck is Educational vs Trade, you ask? Good question. Before we dive into the intricacies of the Educational Market, we'll give a quick overview of children's publishing.

In general terms, children's publishing can be divided into two major categories—the Educational Market and the Trade Market.

The Educational Market sells primarily to schools and libraries (although a shift to adding sales in the Trade Market has noticeably arrived... more on this later). In this market you'll find lots of 4–6 volume series such as *The World's Coldest Climates* or *The Ugliest Edible Insects* or *Coding for Kids.* There is also a huge "behind the scenes" market, with specialty school-related work, like reader's theater, test passages, teacher's guides, and lesson plans.

In contrast, the Trade Market sells books primarily through sales outlets such as Amazon, Barnes and Noble, Books-a-Million, or independent booksellers. This market will also sell to libraries and target schools whenever possible.

Another way to look at it is that educational publishers sell primarily to librarians and teachers. The trade publishers sell most of their books to the end user, the reader.

There is plenty of overlap between the markets. Educational publishers are dabbling further into Trade Market style books and sales outlets. Trade publishers have lots of books targeted to schools. In fact, the irony is how these markets can be so

similar *and* so different depending upon whose perspective you're using, the *reader's* or the *writer's*.

From a *reader's* perspective, the two markets aren't different at all. Both have fiction, non-fiction, poetry, concept books, series, and other products. In fact, young readers happily read books from both markets and never notice a difference.

So why, you wonder, do we care about differentiating between two markets that appear so similar?

Because, as a *writer,* the differences are huge, massive, *ENORMOUS!*

The way that you query, write, revise, and get paid in these two markets is *completely* different. The Educational Market has very strict guidelines on content, reading level, structure, format, and topic. It has a large share of the multi-volume book series you'll find in schools. It's completely different from the Trade Market where you can write whatever you want and hope to sell it on spec. As a writer you'll never "accidentally" sell a book to the Educational Market, while thinking you are selling to the Trade Market, or vice versa. The two markets are as different as wart hogs and jellybeans.

Keeping this in mind, you'll find that each market has advantages and disadvantages. Let's take a *quick look* at a few of these. We'll dig deeper into these differences later in the book. From here on in, we're looking at it from your point of view as a *writer*.

I. QUERIES

Queries in the Educational Market are much more in-volved than in the Trade Market. They require a completely different type of query package. Why is that? Because in the Educational Market you're selling your skills as a writer. You're emphasizing your writing talents, your life experience, your capacity to do research, and your ability to meet dead-lines. You do not send an Educational Publisher a manuscript you're trying to sell (with one notable exception we'll discuss later). Instead, you send a full query package with two or three different writing samples. The editors will check out your samples, decide if they like them, and then get back to you with a project if they're impressed with the way you write.

Compare this to the Trade Market. In the Trade Market you can write whatever type of manuscript you want, then send it off to publishers hoping one will acquire it.

II. THE MANUSCRIPT

After an editor at an educational publisher decides she wants to hire you as a writer, she'll send an assignment via email. It may be a single book, or it may be an offer to write multiple books. It depends upon what the editor needs.

One fascinating part of this process is that editors will frequently offer you projects on topics you know absolutely nothing about!

Mike's first manuscript was a 4,000-word book on gluten. Did he know anything about gluten when he accepted the offer? Heck no! But that didn't stop him.

Sandra's favorite break-in assignment was writing lesson plans for a six-volume e-book series on fast cars. At the time, she thought any vehicle that could outpace a minivan was fast! Working on that series was an eye-opening learning experience!

As you can see, if you want to enter the Educational Market there's a very important rule you'll need to follow—just say YES!

In the Educational Market every assignment comes with lots of rules: word count, number of sidebars, reading level, specific format, and additional notes on the expected art. These will be spelled out in a Manuscript Guidelines document the publisher will send you. Lesson plan jobs come with their own requirements, like vocabulary activities, comprehension questions and references to standards. Everything must align to a specific grade level, curriculum, or standard.

BE CAREFUL WHAT YOU WISH FOR

Taking a project you know nothing about means long hours of research. Add that into your planning!

This is in stark contrast to the Trade Market where you can write a book any way you want. It's a completely different system indeed!

III. PAY AND ROYALTIES

Pay is one area where educational publishing lags. Working for an educational publisher is also known as doing "work for hire." When you're finished, the copyright is no longer yours. The publisher owns all rights. This means they will give you a one-time payment, a single amount that covers your work. It is the only payment you will ever receive. There will be no royalties or additional payments regardless of what sales they generate in the future. The good news is that they do pay quickly because they expect you to write quickly. And if they like you, they'll ask you to do more projects, which can lead to a somewhat steady, if modest, source of income.

On the other hand, the Trade Market pays on a royalty-based system. This is good news if you have a hot-selling book—you'll make money on each sale. But if your book quickly goes out of print, then the advantage isn't as significant.

IV. SPEED TO PUBLICATION

How long does it take to go from signing a contract to seeing your book in print? This is where educational publishing shines. In fact, it truly leaves trade publishing in the dust. The manuscript you submitted to your educational publisher will almost always be on bookshelves in less than a year, perhaps in half that time. This is amazing considering the amount of coordination and logistics required to publish a book, especially one with illustrations or photographs.

One reason for this quick speed to publication is that deadlines are tight and taken very seriously! This isn't the case in the Trade Market.

Publication in the Trade Market is notoriously slow. From the day your manuscript is acquired you can expect to wait

2–2 ½ years before seeing it in a bookstore. Yes. That's a painfully long wait.

V. MARKETING

Marketing is another area where there's a dramatic difference between the two types of publishers. By marketing we mean how a book is introduced, publicized, and sold to potential buyers. Let's first look at the marketing you'll be expected to do with your Educational Market book releases.

Oh wait...there aren't any! None! Nada! Zip! Zilch!

Once you meet your deadline and submit your final polished manuscript to your editor, you are DONE...and ready to begin researching and writing your next Educational Market assignment. In fact, you won't even know your book is released until you get a couple of author copies in the mail.

This absence of being in the spotlight could be ego deflating, but don't let it be. Instead of concentrating on marketing, you can devote your time and energy to your next project. Remember, additional marketing would not be worth it to the author, who doesn't gain any additional pay for increased book sales.

In the Trade Market, the author *actively participates* in the marketing. Or at least they should! For example, your publisher might ask you to connect with your followers on social media, create a short video about your book, present book talks, participate in author interviews for social media or even do book signings. You would *want* to do these, because every additional sale puts money in your pocket (as well as the publisher's).

That's it. That was a quick summary of the differences be-tween the Educational Market and the Trade Market. From here on out we'll be talking about the Educational Market, because that's where you'll be selling your next manuscript!

Comparison of the Educational & Trade Markets*

	TRADE PUBLISHING	EDUCATIONAL PUBLISHING (WORK-FOR-HIRE)
WHO IS THE MARKET?	Individuals	Schools & Libraries Teachers & Librarians
WHO CONCEIVES AND CREATES THE PROJECT?	Author	Publishing Company
WHO OWNS THE COPYRIGHT?	Author	Publishing Company
HOW IS THE AUTHOR PAID?	Advance & Royalties	Flat Fee
WHO MARKETS THE BOOK?	Author & Publisher	Publisher
SPEED TO PUBLICATION	2 to 2.5 years from signed contract	Less than 1 year

*These are generally true, but there are always exceptions depending on the project.

CHAPTER 2

Why You Should Write For The Educational Market

Since you're reading this book, it's likely you've already decided you want to write for the Educational Market. Great! If you're chomping at the bit to get started (Sandra loves trite horse related phrases), then by all means you can skip this chapter and rush along to Chapter 3. However, if you'd like to hear what a great decision you've made, we'll happily massage your ego (and Mike's too, since he thrives on ego boosts) by explaining the great benefits of writing for this market.

I. YOU CAN CHANGE THE WORLD

Let's start by changing the world.

That's right. Changing the world. When you write for the Educational Market, your book will find its way into schools and other educational settings. This is where kids learn. They learn math, science, history, reading, and writing. They build self-awareness, discover how to share ideas, and learn how to interact with others in their community and around the world.

Educational books cover all these topics and more. This is your chance to add your own personal nuggets of wit, wisdom, and worth to the educational system. You'll write books that have a measurable impact on a young reader's learning, literacy, and life. It will be your twist of a phrase or author's perspective that makes a child interested in reading *your* book.

7

It's likely you remember books from your own childhood that made a difference to you.

You might not remember the author or title, but the impact can be lifelong.

Mike remembers voraciously devouring books about airplanes. It led him toward the path of aviation and writing that he's still following today.

Sandra's fascination with joke books and funny stories started early! Laughing out loud seemed an *astounding* way to react to a book! From this, she grasped the power of words *and* the usefulness of books as quirky companions! Both insights continue to shape her writing career.

Writing for the Educational Market can provide these types of personal rewards that aren't as easy to quantify as cashing a check or receiving congratulations for a new book. But knowing you've made a difference in the life of a child is incredibly empowering!

II. FORTUNE AND FAME

Really, you say? Fortune and fame?

Absolutely! We *guarantee* that writing for the Educational Market will lead to fortune and fame!

Well... maybe a little bit. We'll start with fortune. More accurately a very, very small fortune, but who's counting? Pay in the Educational Market might range anywhere from $250 to $2500 for a 500 – 1000 word book. The same is applicable for lesson plans, teacher guides, and test passages (unless you take on a hefty workload in a large curriculum project). In some cases you might manage to top those amounts, but most pay is toward the bottom of this range.

That doesn't sound like much, does it? But the Educational Market is constantly putting out new material. This means educational publishers are always looking for writers. So, if you're a go-getter who actively searches for jobs in this market, you might manage a continuous, though somewhat erratic, flow of money coming in. That can be a nice bonus for your piggy bank.

The fame part of this equation is similar to the fortune. You won't garner any great stardom that makes you an idol with an adoring public, but you *will* officially be a published author. That's a pretty nice place to be. You can show your published book to friends, family and even the occasional stranger. You might be asked to sign a book or pose for a picture. Consider this fame like being a big fish in a small pond. It's kind of fun and might even get you a free cup of coffee.

III. IMPROVE WRITING SKILLS

On a more serious note, there are other advantages to writing for the Educational Market. You will improve your writing skills, become a more disciplined writer, and discover writing resources you might otherwise never have known about.

No matter what type of writer you are, it will add a new level of capability to your writing efforts. The strict guidelines you'll receive with each assignment will improve your research, hone your skills for crafting stories at certain grade levels, and force you to fit your story within tight word limits.

In meeting deadlines, you'll learn to pay attention to your time and effort, then budget both with a new level of thoughtfulness. Likewise, you'll work with resources that will help you along the way—such as text leveling tools and increased use of your thesaurus. These skills and resources are invaluable to any author who is writing for children.

Mike is the perfect example. A year after his entry into the Educational Market, he honed his skills enough to figure out how to write better manuscripts for the Trade Market. This led to the acquisition of six manuscripts by trade publishers over the next three years. Without his newfound knowledge from the Educational Market, the manuscripts never would have sold.

Sandra did the same. She took her years of writing for educational publishers and parlayed them into writing nonfiction stories for the Trade Market as well as selling an

QUICK SUCCESS

Having your own published hardcover book *in-hand* within 9 months of accepting a project is a great feeling!

informational fiction series to Astra publishing (co-written with her sidekick, Mike).

Not bad, huh? By writing for the Educational Market you're getting paid to improve your writing skills, while putting out terrific books that kids will love. And, it can increase your potential for selling in the Trade Market.

Wow!

CHAPTER 3

Which Educational Market Publisher Fits You?

While we firmly stand by our earlier advice to say *yes* to any job assignment—even those that stretch your comfort zone (i.e. gluten and fast cars)—setting yourself up to succeed before you've said yes is also smart. Put simply, you'll want to target your energy and efforts toward specific educational publishers that seem to be a good fit for *you*. Pitch your services to publishers who speak to *your* expertise, knowledge, interests, and passions.

Think of it like dating. If you're interested in music, art, and nature, you don't want to be stuck with someone who only talks about engines, race cars, and computers. I'm sure plenty of you have been *there* before. Yuck! Sorry if we've dredged up any repressed memories.

But leaving the nuances of our personal lives behind, let's take a closer look some characteristics of Educational Market publishers.

I. THE HEART AND SOUL OF PUBLISHERS

Each Educational Publisher is unique. Some may emphasize history and social sciences, focusing on nonfiction about people, places, and events. *Women of the American Revolution* or *New Views on Ancient Civilizations* might be some of the series found in their catalogues.

or *New Views on Ancient Civilizations* might be some of the series found in their catalogues.

Another publisher might focus on STEAM topics (Science, Technology, Engineering, Art, and Math). They would publish books like *Energy, Weather, Nutrition,* and the *Solar System.*

Some publishers produce activity and how-to books that feature experiments, crafts, or journaling activities. Others will be heavy on fictional zombie, ghost, and detective series.

What, you ask? Zombies and educational publishers go together? Yes! It's true. Despite the incongruity, we did mention *fictional series* and *educational publishers* in the same breath. However, fiction is a smaller segment of the market and tends to be more difficult to break into.

But that's not all. Some educational publishers want materials other than books. These include projects like student study guides and specialized test preparation. The opportunities are vast!

All Educational Market publishers—from very large multi-subject publishers to smaller, highly specialized ones—will have a distinguishable feel based on the type of content they publish. This content often speaks to the heart and soul of their mission, driving their publishing decisions.

If you spend your free time musing over mathematical mysteries, you'll want to align yourself with a publisher who has a vibrant STEAM collection. If you remain traumatized by your botched science fair volcano in 5th grade, you may want to move on to a publisher that needs poetry. For those of you who happily tour historical sites on your family vacations, that's a hint you should try to work with publishers who produce rich history or travel series.

Identifying what you *really* want is an essential first step in finding the proper fit.

Once that's accomplished, you can align your interests to particular subjects and publishers. At least that's what we attempt to do in a perfect world.

So back to our dating analogy. If you're hoping to write fictional stories about zombies and detectives, you don't want

YOUR CAREER PATH

The Trade Market may not be your end game. *Many* writers embrace the unique features of the Educational Market and build steady careers staying put.

to engage with the publisher that focuses on research-laden nonfiction topics. That's a date that won't end well.

The caveat? Life isn't perfect. Despite your best efforts you'll find yourself offered a project that doesn't quite fit. Think of it as a "life experience" or "paying your dues." It may not be the perfect manuscript, but getting a toehold in the market is a huge step on your writing journey. This is where you take an insightful look at yourself and decide exactly what you can do. Are you ready to put in 20 hours of research and 20 hours of writing for a 1,000 word manuscript that's due in three weeks? Can you meet a 45-day deadline for your series of three zombie manuscripts, written to a third-grade level? If you're truly interested in the Educational Market, this is where it's time to be bold and take the leap! You'll discover this market provides you with months of boredom between jobs, and then has you writing frantically once an email offer appears in your inbox.

If you decide to say "YES, I'll do anything," then buckle your seatbelt! Mr. Toad's Wild Ride will be a lazy jaunt in the park compared to your new adventure. This is the path Mike found himself on...impatient to get books published, *no matter what!*

When Mike began his attempts to enter the Educational Market, his mantra was very simple—*say yes to every single thing that comes my way.* It's a road lined with long hours of research and low pay. *But,* and this is a very significant *but,* it quickly teaches you the ropes of the Educational Market, and sets you up to choose better assignments in the future. Not only that, you'll likely have a book out in less than a year!

II. WHAT'S THEIR ANGLE?

One characteristic that might attract you to one publisher over another is *how* they cover a subject or topic. What approach does the publisher use? Do they include elements that appeal to you in unique ways? What caused you to pause as you perused their catalogue or flipped through their books?

Try to identify those things you like or dislike about a publisher's books. Sandra recalls a young-reader series that blended biographies with time travel and tasty treats. Talk about a delectable combination! In each volume, two main characters traveled to a bakery, ice-cream shop, or some such epicurean setting. That's where they met historic figures who shared details of their achievements while at the same time enjoying tasty tidbits. She loved the unusual concoction of elements in the series and knew she wanted to write for this publisher. This led her to pitch Rourke Educational Media. Three months later she received an assignment to write two early-reader fiction books. Sweet indeed!

In another instance, Sandra wanted to work with Rosen Publishing. They were producing high-interest collections of nonfiction books like *If We Had Wings: The Story of the Tuskegee Airmen; Cherokee Heroes: Three Who Made a Difference;* and *Colonial Life and the Revolutionary War in New York.* Sandra knew students enjoyed these types of high-interest titles, which also improved their reading skills. She wanted to be a part of that potent combination. Sandra approached the publisher by pitching teacher materials to supplement the books. Although they turned down that pitch, it opened doors that led to other projects—lots of other projects! Sandra continues to work extensively with Rosen on instructional projects of all forms and size!

Mike had a similar experience with Heinemann Publishing. After sending a sample of his poetry, it turned out they were looking for silly fictional poems for third and fourth graders. Score! That happens to be one of Mike's core strengths. This happy confluence of publisher need and writer ability led to a wonderful collaboration of books.

So, identifying the *style* of books a publisher produces, and focusing on those that match your strengths, can increase your odds of gaining entry into the Educational Marketplace.

But never feel limited to only one publisher.

Thankfully, as a writer you're allowed more than one partner! This shouldn't be attempted with our dating analogy, but it does hold true for educational publishing. In this industry it makes good sense to build solid relationships with two or more educational publishers.

II. FINDING YOUR PUBLISHERS

"Wait a minute!" you say.

We've told you to search for the heart and soul of a publisher and to figure out what their angle is. But, after a thorough search of the internet, you haven't found any author/publisher dating apps to make it easy! Nor do the educational publishers put this important information in a convenient author/publisher matching program. What the heck! The truth is there's simply no easy way to do it.

So how exactly can you figure out what different publishers are like?

We're glad you asked.

First, you could go to the nearest drinking establishment and hunker up to the bar. Then yell out, "I need an educational publisher!" We haven't actually tried this ourselves, but we're very curious as to how it might work out! Make sure to have a friend get it all on video for your future social media promotions.

PUBLISHER COMPATIBILITY

Don't fret! You'll likely know a compatible publisher when you see one. Take your time studying their catalogues.

Our next suggestion is more prosaic. Research. Research. Research. Remember we mentioned you'd be *honing* your research skills? Your honing begins now, as you start researching the educational publishers themselves! In this chapter we'll break it down into a "quick and dirty" plan specific to finding the best publishers for you. In Chapter 8 we'll provide a plan for researching the *projects* you'll be working on.

Let's dive in and find your match. It's a simple three step process. Get ready to swipe right.

STEP 1

Obtain a list of Educational Market publishers. There are a few great places to do this.

- Use this simple Publishers List
  - Here are 30 educational publishers listed by name only. You can do an internet search to find them online. Once you get there, check out their books and see what type appeals to you. Then, look for their submission guidelines page. If they don't have one, the information may be in the FAQ's. As a last ditch effort, if you can't find submission guidelines anywhere, simply email their information page and ask how you can become a writer for them.

EDUCATIONAL MARKET PUBLISHERS

ABC-CLIO	Capstone	APass*
Abdo	Cengage Group	Aptara*
Amicus	The Creative Company	ATP Assessments*
Annick Press	Heinemann	Publishing Solutions Group*
Arbordale	Little Fox	The Research Masters*
Arcadia Publishing	Pearson	Six Red Marbles*
Bearport Publishing	Quarto	Straive*
Black Rabbit Books	Red Line Editorial	Teacher Created Materials*
Blue Dot Kids Press	Rosen	Teaching Point*
Cavendish Square	Rourke Educational Media	Westchester Educational Services*

Groups specializing in Teacher Materials, Lesson Plans & Assessment Materials

---

- Join the SCBWI
  - *The Essential Guide to Publishing for Children* has a treasure trove of submission information, and is published by the SCBWI. If you aren't a member yet, we highly suggest you join today. You'll get access to *The Essential Guide to Publishing for Children* as well as a wide range of other great information and

support in this wonderful and highly respected children's writers' community.
- *The Children's Writers and Illustrators Market*
  - The hardcopy edition is updated every year. It also includes online access to get the most current information.
- Search Online
  - You can always do your own search for educational publishers. If you do this, be careful. There are plenty of scammers who will take your money to do something you could easily do on your own. In fact, you should *never* spend any money doing online research!

But enough of that. Once you've noted a few publishers, head on down to step two.

STEP 2

Look at books from publishers that appeal to you.

The best way to get quick, up-to-the-minute information, is to go to the publisher's website and search for catalogues. You'll typically find these divided into spring and fall volumes. Download the two most recent catalogues.

Scan through the books and find ones that appeal to you. Then, copy the title and find it on Amazon where you can "look inside" a few pages. This will give you a good indication of the writing style and reading level of the book.

Another way to look inside some educational books is to make a friend who's an elementary school teacher or librarian. Get her to invite you to her school library. There you can look at educational series on the shelves and note publishers who produce the books you like. You'll be able to gauge a large selection of books in a short period of time this way.

STEP 3

Keep a list!

Since you're doing all this work, it behooves you to keep a list of publishers and the books you liked. Don't forget to note the imprint of the book, which typically denotes the reading level of the series. This way you'll be able to reference their imprints when pitching your wares to the appropriate publishers. Don't lose your list!

CHAPTER 4

WRITING OPPORTUNITIES

If you want to connect with compatible publishers, you should start by asking a few questions about yourself. This would be like filling out your profile on our hypothetical dating app.

What exactly, do you *want* to write about? What age level will you write for? What are you an expert in? What hobbies do you have? What type of manuscripts do you *enjoy* writing?

Make sure to answer these questions honestly. Filling out a profile with bad information will only lead to bad matches—and who wants that!

Let's start with the *what?* What do you want to write. Consider a few of your choices. This is not an all-inclusive list, but it covers a large segment of your opportunities.

NONFICTION: social studies, history, science, language arts, math, business, careers, physical education, sports, other.

FICTION: realistic fiction, mystery, fantasy, science fiction, reader's theater, drama, poetry, letters, essays, themes, other.

TEACHER RELATED MATERIALS: reading passages, test questions, student lesson plans, teacher guides, student study guides, other.

Take a minute to think about it... Okay. Time's up. Those of you who want to write *nonfiction* raise your hands.

I. NONFICTION

Hurrah! *Winner. Winner. Money for dinner!*

Maybe that's not exactly the quote you've heard before, but it makes sense here. We have *great news* for those of you with your hands in the air! Nonfiction is a large segment of the Educational Market. You'll have a superb chance at breaking into educational publishing in this research intensive, photo-illustrated, nonfiction category. These opportunities are available at almost every educational publisher.

This large segment of the Educational Market will be your most likely place to find a writing opportunity. Photo-illustrated nonfiction is generally written in a series of 4-6 books, with titles like *Gargantuan Insects* or *Plants of the Tropical Forests* or *Space Exploration.* Search for different grade levels, topics and publishers. This is how you'll find the publishers and grade levels that best fit your writing style.

If you're an expert in something, say motorcycles or gardening or dancing, then this could be your 'foot in the door' into life as a published author. If a publisher is looking for your particular skill, you might find yourself in the right place at the right time.

FACT OR FICTION

Do you want to write both? You may be able to flex your nonfiction and fiction writing muscles in the Education Market. Unlike in the Trade Market, you're not building an author brand so there's more flexibility in flip-flopping.

II. FICTION

Fictional work in the Educational Market is also generally written in a series of books, typically 3 in a series. But no photos here. Fiction books have simple illustrations that grab the attention of young readers. Topics might range from detective stories to friendship, from zombies to pet dragons.

This smaller segment of the market allows more creativity in writing and less time spent on research. It also typically pays better than photo-illustrated nonfiction.

In mathematical terms, Fiction = More Author Creativity + More Pay + Less Research, which also = More Difficult to Break

Into. Lots of authors want to break into this segment of the market. It's harder to find projects like these until you're already established, but it's well worth trying!

The fiction market also has subcategories. A few of the larger ones include poetry, reader's theater, and graphic novels. Writing a reader's theater play is completely different than writing a fictional story on vampire zombies. Writing poetry is different than writing a clue-based whodunit. Writing graphic novels deserves an entire book on its own, but it's not something we'll be focusing on here. Just keep in mind, the opportunity does exist, and it's a huge one.

As you can see from these few examples, there is plenty of variety in fiction. The downside is the added difficulty of breaking into this market.

III. TEACHER RELATED PRODUCTS

Another huge, but less publicized segment of the Educational Market, is teacher related products. If you're a teacher or in-the-know in any way within the educational system, there are a huge variety of projects you might be assigned. These include devising test questions, writing passages, making study guides, or designing prototypes for new school-related programs. The possibilities are wide and varied. These projects can be more difficult to find, but if you're interested, search out publishers that specialize in these lesser known projects. Six Red Marbles, Rosen Publishing, and Straive are a few publishers that fit the bill.

IV. WHAT READING LEVEL WILL YOU WRITE FOR?

Another decision you'll need to make is what grade levels you'd like to write for. Mike's sweet spot is grades 2–4, though he'll dabble on either side of that. His least favorite manuscript dealt with gluten, written for a 6th grade audience. The lesson he learned? Don't stray too far outside of your comfort zone unless you're willing to put in a lot of work!

Sandra's favorites are grades 2–4 as well, though she also likes working at the PreK–Grade 1 levels. This young crowd is eager to read, yet their developing skills can be tricky to finesse. Even though these jobs are often smaller (less word count) and require less research, writing engaging prose for the youngest readers still takes time and effort. The lesson Sandra learned?

Once you've developed some know-how in this market, always weigh the demands on your time against the value of the job.

Also, if you're interested in writing lessons plans that require grade-level expertise on topics such as phonics, do NOT misjudge your skills. This could easily reduce the quality of your work and increase the amount of time you spend writing.

For those of you interested in writing above the K–5 grade levels, it's a bit beyond the scope of this book. However, there's high demand for those who can comfortably write for these older students and readers. Well-written, engaging work will find a place across all grade levels and all types of products— from nonfiction books to teacher lesson plans.

However, there *is* one segment of this market that reaches out to older, progressing, readers with high-interest content (grades 6–12) and low reading levels (grades 3 or 4). The books in this special niche are referred to as hi-lo books. Hi-lo means high interest topics that older readers want to read about, but written at a lower reading level to help them understand the content and improve their reading skills. These opportunities abound, no matter the grade level that sparks your interest!

That's it. You've taken the first step to lifelong happiness… determining what you really want! Now that you have an idea what you're looking for, it's time to settle comfortably in front of your computer and make that dream come true!

V. DON'T HOLD OUT FOR THE PERFECT PROJECT

BUT...regardless of which type of writing you prefer, it's important to note that your quickest path to publication is to volunteer to write *anything!* We are reemphasizing this point because it's crucial! Being a desperate, motivated, enthusiastic writer is the role you're most likely to succeed in. Once your foot is in the door, you'll be able to slowly work your way into projects more appropriate to your temperament, skills, and hopefully, with a better pay scale. Good luck!

KEEP IT SIMPLE

If you decide to write in the K-4 grade level always simplify your writing. You'll be using short simple sentences and basic vocabulary throughout.

CHAPTER 5

Your Submission Package

"Toto, I've a feeling we're not in Kansas anymore."

Dorothy made this powerful and iconic statement after she began submitting to the Educational Market. We're pretty sure.

If you've dabbled in submitting your work to the Trade Market, you can ignore all of your hard-earned knowledge from that process—at least while submitting to educational publishers. Educational publishing has its own set of unique rules that you must follow, beginning with your *Submission Package*.

This package is also called an *Introductory Packet,* because it introduces your desires, interests, and skills—similar to an online profile you'd set up if you were looking for a perfect match! Woo hoo!

Welcome to the Wonderful World of Educational Publishing!

Let's start by answering the most important question—what the heck is a submission package? Shouldn't you simply write a story and send it out?

The answer to that question is...NO!

To describe an Educational Market submission package in snobbish hyperbole, it's a meticulously devised compilation of specialized documents, time-consuming in their preparation and crucial in their components and subject matter.

Oops. That line was for our other book... *How to make Entry into the Educational Market as Difficult as Possible.* But now back to our regularly scheduled program.

At an educational publisher your submission package is a combination of three separate items.

1. **A Query Letter**
2. **A Resume**
3. **Two or More Writing Samples**

The bad news? This package will take lots of time and refined writing skills to complete properly. The good news? You only need to do it once! Yay!! This submission package, or introductory packet, will suffice for most publishers with only minor modifications.

Regardless of the term used, let there be no doubt—these documents must be meticulously prepared because they will ultimately determine if you land a writing assignment! The time you spend working on a great submission package will pay you back over and over.

The submission package is chock full of carefully prepared materials that showcase your writing talents, life experience, capacity to do research, and your ability to meet deadlines. Phew, that's a lot of stuff! Which is why a submission package requires *three* uniquely different items.

Before you run and hide in the closet—pause, breathe, and don't worry. We'll describe each part of your submission package, show you samples, and guide you step-by-step through the process of creating your own. We'll also discuss tailoring your approach to specific publishers, which is a must-follow rule if you're submitting specialized content.

SAMPLE QUERY LETTERS

Samples appear in the Appendix.

I. QUERY LETTER

The first item in your submission package is the query letter. This letter is a hello, a quick introduction, a few notes about yourself, and a statement about your desire to write for the publisher. It's your *first impression,* the first showcase of your writing ability. It can determine whether an editor reads the other parts of your package or hits the delete key. This extremely important document will be an editor's first impression of you, like meeting your date for the first time (you knew this comparison was coming!). While you may dislike the idea that your big writing opportunity relies on a quick fifteen-second first impression, that's how the system works. Editors are always on the lookout for skilled, engaging, enthusiastic writers. Show them that's exactly who you are by impressing the heck out of them in your query letter.

How do you impress an editor? First, don't make any stupid errors. No misspelling or poor formatting, and especially don't send a *personalized* query to the wrong publisher.

You'll also need to research the publisher and reference a nugget of information you've gleaned about their books. Let them know your decision to submit to their company was thoughtful and intentional, not just one in a haphazard scattershot of queries. Personalize your query by doing one of the following:

- Mention the imprint you'd like to write for.
- Discuss any experience you've had with their titles. You may be a teacher who uses them in class or a parent who's read them at the school library.
- Comment on their mission statement or motto.

DON'T STRESS ON FORMATTING

The *content* of your query is what's important. Don't stress about how you format the date or other minor details.

This simple personalization goes a long way. It showcases your ability to do research and your motivation to work for that particular publisher. But don't overdo it!

If you're like Sandra, who can gush and gush, reign in your effusive instincts! This would only alarm your editor and start her thinking about restraining orders! Keep the tone professional—a kind of business casual! You're looking for a quick hook in the beginning of your letter, not setting yourself up to be a stalker.

Your query is concise, professional, and shows your knowledge of the company.

You will also want to introduce your "writing self" to them—*briefly!* Your bio will follow later, but a quick note here can set the hook. If you've published something before, include a detail or two about your books or articles. Note any highlights that show you're a good fit for that publisher. If you haven't published a book before, that's fine, but don't mention it. Remember, they'll be looking at your writing samples to determine if they like your work.

Next comes a few words about your job. Regardless of what you do, you are an expert at your job! It doesn't matter if you're a fast-food worker, a nurse, a janitor, a coach, or a pilot. Your skill set may be exactly what the publisher is looking for.

Those of you who work with children or have jobs in the educational system get bonus points! Educational publishers love teachers, administrators, teaching aides, or anyone with a child-centric job. If you know about curriculum standards, even better. Mention it! But avoid using jargon or acronyms.

You'll also want to mention your ability to work with schedules and meet deadlines. Mike's queries include the statement "As a former military officer I'm comfortable working with tight schedules and meeting deadlines." No beating around the bush there!

Sandra deals with the subject another way. She explains she's a teacher and adds that she can still dedicate 20 hours per week to writing and will meet all deadlines. This sends the message that she's thought this through and can manage it, even with a full-time job.

The bottom line? Offer a short, sweet statement like "I can work within tight schedules and understand the importance of meeting all deadlines." Chatting about schedules, deadlines, and turnaround time is the kind of sweet talk that will make you irresistible to an Educational Market editor!

Your query will be electronic, typically written in the body of an email. Your resume and writing samples may follow in the body of your email or be attached as a word document. Any requirements you need to know about submitting your materials are spelled out in the publisher's submission guidelines. The query (and everything else!) should be free of common social media abbreviations, emojis, and other informal devices. This is a professional document showing you know how to write. Once you're established with an editor, then bring on the emojis to your heart's content.

Important note! Write your query in a word document and transfer it to email only when you're completely finished!

Writing and editing your query within the body of an email is a very bad idea. On a related note, *never* insert the editor's email address until your email draft is completely finished—to include query *and* attachments! Most writers have had the unpleasant experience of sending an email without their manuscripts attached. This requires sending a second email to the editor saying how you already messed up! Editors are not impressed by this lack of professionalism, and it's certainly not a great way to start a new career.

Although most publishers simply need an email query and word document attachment, others use specialized electronic submission platforms. If you find one of those, simply follow the directions. They may require a query and writing samples or something else specific that is clearly spelled out. No matter, the rule remains the same—follow their rules!

When addressing a typical query letter, feel free to use an editor's name if you have one, even if you found it in one of your resources listings Otherwise, a simple "Dear Submissions Editor" works fine. Avoid a highly formal salutation like "To Whom it may Concern." That's unusual in this industry.

Remember—*very important*—to carefully tailor your query to each publisher. While the overall structure remains the same, you'll have to adapt the content.

II. RESUME

The next puzzle piece in your submission package is your resume.

GREAT! you say. You already have a current resume on file! In fact, you recently spent hours updating it and it's polished to perfection! You might, at this very moment, be tap dancing around your desk because you're thrilled you won't have to put in the additional work to finish a new resume!

Insert *SCREEEEEEECH* sound and let's gently bring a note about resumes to your attention. In the world of educational publishing, we're not talking about a *typical* job resume! In this case, we're talking about a non-traditional, uniquely focused,

SAMPLE RESUMES

Samples appear in the Appendix.

life skills and knowledge resume that will land you assignments in educational publishing. We recognize this may be shocking news if you thought resumes differed only in fonts, format, and the archaic category of paper quality. However, it will make more sense when you see the type of information that's used to land your educational writing assignment.

Let's start by slipping inside the head of a typical editor at a typical educational publishing company. She has just left a meeting where, after many painstaking months of planning, their new season of projects has been finalized. Due to the sheer volume of projects (maybe one or two hundred) and the tight production schedule, she is eager to begin assigning writers to books. The company's exciting new series include: Quirky Underwater Creatures, Careers in the Arts, What's Next in Gaming Technology, Environmental Disasters, Repurposed Craft Projects for Kids, and many more.

How will the editor assign these projects? That's where your resume comes in. Your resume lists the skills, knowledge and experience you have gained throughout your life. If you're an undersea photographer, you'll be first in line for the *Quirky Underwater Creatures* series. If you're a national video game champion, the *What's Next in Gaming Technology* is yours. If your favorite hobby is crafting, you'll find an offer for *Repurposed Craft Projects for Kids* in your email.

The editor doles out job assignments, hoping her match-making efforts will ensure a timely receipt of high-quality manuscripts. In general, this is how the process works.

Your resume is a tackle box of shiny objects—your expertise, experiences, and interests—used to lure an editor with her broad, unusual, and complex needs.

On the flip side of this perfect world, many of these projects will *not* have a great author match, but they still need to be written. This is why you may ultimately find an offer in your email to write *Pickles Around the World* or *Why Toads Have Warts.* The bottom line? You'll possibly be offered a dreamy topic you wished for, but you should also count on a few quirky surprises!

By now, you're likely cozying up to the fact that preparing this kind of *special* resume takes a different mindset than preparing a traditional work resume. Here, you want to showcase YOU, so an editor can easily find your "fit" among their forthcoming line up of books. You'll want to include everything that makes you unique as an individual and shows that you're well-suited to author books on a variety of subjects.

Some categories you'll want to include:

- **Education** - If it's significant, include it. Note any specialized training, certification courses, and college or post graduate degrees. Any of these can make you a subject matter expert. For instance, your degree in English Literature would be an asset if you wanted to write curriculum guides for the literary classics. If you don't have any specialized education, that's not a problem either. It's simply something you won't mention.
- **Expertise** – List anything you're knowledgeable about. This is generally based on practical experience—such as your nursing career, your work on rebuilding motorcycles, your years in martial arts, certifications you've received attending space camp, or your 7-year stint raising pet pot-bellied pigs.
- **Child Centric Experiences** - This category showcases your kid-friendly activities. It includes any paid or volunteer experiences with children, such as school experience, home-schooling, special instruction (work with English-language learners, etc.), volunteering at a library, tutoring, working with scouting programs, sports coaching, or other similar activities.
- **Interests/Hobbies** – If you enjoy doing something in your spare time, list it! Do you collect coins, marbles, or hand-painted china? Maybe you compete in sand-castle building or pogo-stick jumping competitions. Perhaps you juggle, perform magic tricks, and ride unicycles. Here, you're going to highlight your interests or hobbies—even the quirkier ones.
- **Published Writing** – If you are a published author, then list it. This includes any paid or unpaid writing. It might be geared for children or adults, informative or narrative

WHAT TO LIST FIRST?

The order of your categories is also flexible.

writing, online writing—any kind of published writing counts. This could also include formal editing, proofreading, or any other writing-based activities. Have you published an article in a magazine, written and posted a blog, proofread newsletters? All of these count.

You can use these categories, or one of your own, in your educational resume. Perhaps you want to list Field Experiences (to tout environmental research strengths), or Medical Certifications (if you wish to land health & safety assignments). There isn't a standard style, so you have lots of flexibility in determining how best to showcase YOU!

In case you're wondering, there's no need to include a list of work-related or personal references. Nor do you need to include start and end dates of activities. While both are commonly used in traditional resumes, they are not necessary here.

Your resume should be short and concise. No more than two pages. Capitalize main topics. Use bulleted lists. Avoid lengthy sentences and in-depth descriptions. Use a standard 12-point font. Ample white space is inviting.

Preparing your resume will take time and brainstorming power. It's likely you haven't ever needed to list your quirky skills alongside your educational qualifications and knowledge base. Enjoy the process! It'll be eye-opening and fun as you celebrate the *you* that *you've* become!

III. WRITING SAMPLES

WRITING SAMPLES

Samples appear in the Appendix.

Now it's time to use an epicurean analogy—refreshing, right!

Your query and resume will whet the appetite of the Editor, but your writing samples are the main course. You *must* make sure these samples are full of prime ingredients like tenderloin steak and roasted asparagus, or sizzling tofu and quinoa if you're vegetarian. Don't deliver a batch of sour grapes!

The editor *wants* to admire your impressive writing skills. She wants to see your command of craft and your distinctive style. Keep in mind that your grasp of the Educational Market is also on display. This means your samples must show strong, solid writing for children at particular grade levels. Write your samples at the grade level you want to write for the publisher. Everything—the manner and style in which you cover a topic—must be grade-level appropriate. Do not include an adult level writing sample!

For example, a nonfiction writing sample on the eruption of Mt. Vesuvius in 79 CE will look and feel very different for readers in 2nd grade, 4th grade, and 7th grade. Vocabulary, sentence structure, and even the content will differ among the grade level samples. The same is true for a fictional story. All the elements—characters, setting, plot, dialogue—must be prepared with a specific grade level in mind.

In your writing samples, show them your writing chops, while keeping your reader in mind.

We know what you're thinking. What if you're clueless about writing at various grade levels? Don't worry! That's how we all started. Besides, you already know that older kids use bigger words and younger kids use smaller words—you're halfway there! To take you the rest of the way, we've explained the *leveling* process in detail in Chapter 9. Leveling is the art of writing to a particular reading level. We'll also discuss the ATOS and Lexile measurement systems which are used to check your work. These two great tools show the reading level of your manuscript. You'll use them to gauge and adjust your writing to the level you need. Also, your leveling conundrum will be short lived. You'll quickly master the art of leveled writing once you're crafting your fourth or fifth assignment! Guaranteed!

Aha! Several of you are raising your hands, probably with the same question in mind. You noticed we titled this section *Writing Samples,* using the plural form. Yes, we did. So exactly how many samples are we talking about?

A rule of thumb is to include at least two writing samples in your query. Two samples is sparse, and an absolute minimum. Three or four samples would be the sweet spot, while more than five samples is overkill. Mike uses three. Sandra often uses four.

WRITING SAMPLE LEVEL

No need to worry about the ATOS or Lexile level of your sample writing. Simply make sure your samples are written for kids and not adults. Simpler is better.

What do these include? Always include a nonfiction manuscript. Nonfiction is the bread-and-butter of educational publishers. If you're interested in writing fiction, include a fiction sample too. If you're interested in a specialty assignment, like reader's theater or poetry, include a sample of that. Finally, if you're planning to write at highly varying grade levels, like first grade and fifth grade, include a sample of each.

Your research from an earlier chapter (where you checked out different publishers) should help guide your decisions about what to write. Going back to our dating analogy, focus your topics on shared interests so the experience is enjoyable for both of you. A best-case scenario is to prepare samples specifically for the publishers you've deemed a "good fit." However, you'll want a couple "generic samples," or basic nonfiction manuscripts that fit the needs of all educational publishers. This will make it easier to fill out your submissions package without having to write a multitude of manuscripts.

IV. UNEDITED WRITING

There's an interesting comment you'll notice when submitting writing samples. The guidelines typically specify *unedited writing samples only*. Do *NOT* take this to heart. What they mean is *unpublished* writing samples; samples that have not been edited by a *publisher*. You definitely *must* edit your sample... a lot! Send it through your critique group and revise as necessary, again and again if required. It needs to be fully polished and ready to go before you send it off. Just don't use any previously *published* writing.

V. PUBLISHER SPECIFIED SAMPLES

Some publishers add a personal twist to submission samples. They may have a system in place for soliciting samples and collecting your biographical details as Sandra discovered during her early research into educational markets. At the time, she contacted Millbook Press and received a "writing packet" that asked for specific writing samples (broad subject area and grade level). The samples were based on their forthcoming needs. Publishers might also put out a *Call for Authors*—or post a *Work for Hire request* on social media or on sites frequented by writers (which are provided later in this book).

When this happens, they may have specific guidelines for their samples. Make sure to follow their directions exactly! Completing samples in the way they requested—and meeting all their requirements—shows you can do exactly the work they want.

VI. WORD COUNT

If you are not already a word-count afficionado, you will be soon. In no time, you'll be able to eyeball everything you write and, with great precision, shout out its word count: "250 words! 1500 words! 12,500 words!" Why? Because size really, really matters in the publishing industry. Which means word count is also important to us writers—at least if we want to be published! Sticking to word count tops every educational writer's "Must Do List"—along with meeting deadlines. So let's dive head first into your new obsession with word count, beginning with your writing samples.

Good things come in small packages, particularly in your writing samples. Mike's rule of thumb is that *every* sample should be 500 words or less. No exceptions. Sandra uses the same 500-word limit, although she may occasionally allow up to 700 words for fiction. Both methods work fine.

Each typical writing sample is an entire story with a beginning and an end (complete with a narrative arc if it's fiction), all written in the tight word count noted. Writing these is samples not for the faint of heart! A quick aside here for teachers or educators. If you're pitching lesson plans, your samples should be two to three pages, single spaced.

However, there is an exception to the "entire story" type of sample. If you're planning on writing longer works of fiction, it's okay to use an excerpt, like the first chapter of your manu-script, as one of your samples. Try to keep it to one page, single spaced, never longer than two pages. That means about 500 words, never more than 1,000.

In the good news department, working with a tight word count makes for simple formatting. One standard page—with one-inch margins, single spaced lines, and 12 point font—consists of about 500 words. Yes. We did say single spaced lines. This is one of the only times you'll send any editor a story that is single spaced!

In general, one page per story is all the space you'll have to flaunt your stuff! Editors want to get a sense of your engaging style and voice *and* they want to see how well you can execute a crisp, cohesive work with a limited word count.

VII. WHAT EDITORS LOOK FOR

NONFICTION

Now that we've clarified the word count, let's take a quick glance at what your writing sample needs in order to be competitive.

For nonfiction, editors will be looking for:
- An engaging hook
- Sub-headings with exciting new facts.
- A concise conclusion, preferably with some sort of twist.

Your nonfiction sample must show an ability to select topics and express key ideas effectively. And lest you forget—all in 500 words or less!

ENGAGE 'EM AT THE GET GO

Hook the editor right away! Busy editors simply scan your samples. Rely on your publisher research to cast the perfect editorial lure.

FICTION

For fiction, editors will be looking for:
- An engaging hook.
- A conflict, problem, or issue to deal with.
- Unfolding events that keep the reader interested.
- A satisfying ending—twist, surprise, lesson learned, or other?

Here, you're showing you can write a typical story arc—a beginning, rising action, and a conclusion—in a tight 700 words (or within 500 words if Mike is writing it).

POETRY

Let's move on to poetry. The rule here is simple...make sure it's engaging, lyrical, and *amazing!* Editors receive many attempts at poetry that are, let's say, less than overwhelming. The fact is—poetry is very difficult to write well.

Before sending this type of sample, know what kind of poetry the publisher is looking for and ensure that *yours* is appropriate and well-written. It's not as easy as it sounds.

As authors, we like our own writing. Our poetry flows smoothly onto the page and sounds amazing when we read it to ourselves. Unfortunately, it may not flow as smoothly to other readers. Putting it another way, it's easy to write poor poetry. Poems that sound good to the author can sound like a cat yowling at the moon to other readers. This is especially problematic when sending in writing samples.

Let's say an editor reads a nonfiction sample and thinks, hmmm, not bad. She isn't hooked yet, but she thinks the author might have potential. Then she reads a poorly written poem. She's totally unimpressed.

This sample poem has the potential to shift her opinion about the author's overall writing abilities.

It could turn a thumbs up into a thumbs down.

But what if your poetry is good? Then definitely, send a sample! Once again, make sure it's written at the appropriate reading level. If you're tempted to include different forms, such as haiku and limericks and multiple stanza cinquains, you might want to rethink your agenda. A simple lyrical poem written at the proper reading level will grab the editor's attention.

Mike writes a lot of poetry. In his samples he sticks to couplets and stanzas, although they do have varied rhyme schemes to avoid singsong-like repetition. He also dabbles in other styles of poetry when writing actual manuscripts, despite not knowing the difference between a cinquain and a sonnet! He also thought the word *stanza* meant *four related lines in a poem.* Sandra has since explained that this is more accurately called a quatrain. Oops.

But to get back on topic, how much poetry should you include? One page with one or two poems is fine. Two pages is overkill. Make sure the poems are grade level appropriate. Editors do not want to read adult level poetry when selecting writers for kids. As a word of caution, if you're planning to indulge in risky poetic behavior, make it good! Your limerick had better be hilariously funny at a kid level...not adult! Your haiku should be worthy of the National Poets Haiku award, kid's division. Otherwise, stick to a simple, easily read-aloud rhyme pattern. The editor is gauging your level of expertise with a hyper critical eye. Don't mistake her as your supportive critique partner who loves your bold forays into the unknown!

VIII. LESSON PLANS

Calling all teachers. Calling all teachers. Here's a section of the book you don't want to sleep through—educational publishing made especially for you—*lesson plans!* They may not have the panache of poetry or the flair of fiction, but they *could* provide a path to steady income—dollars to your door.

Educational publishers produce many of the lesson plans found in our school systems. Here's a chance to make a few dollars while simultaneously contributing to the way our children learn.

If you're interested in this venue, then your lesson plan should be concise. It must clearly demonstrate your insights with lesson design and delivery. Samples can address reading development or comprehension skills. They might also link to science, social studies, or math. Feel free to adapt materials from a great lesson you've delivered in the past.

Your sample might get a closer look if you show your skills with lessons that help struggling learners, or those whose primary language is not English. Just like any other submission, lesson plans should reflect the specialties of your targeted publishers and shine with enough know-how to impress an editor. But don't get into so much detail that you drag them into the weeds.

For lesson plans, editors will be looking for:
- Basic Components - title, objective, standards, and a step-by-step lesson: opening activity, direct instruction,

practice, a closing, and ways to differentiate.
- Approach and Content – compatible with current norms and curricula.
- Tone and Language - teacher-friendly, on grade level, and reflecting the style of the publisher.

Limit each lesson plan sample to no more than three pages, with headings for major elements and lots of white space between sections for easy reading. An editor will scan them looking for the basics. If they don't say how many to submit, stick with about four. This will give an editor a good sense of your skill in all the main content areas. If you're writing at higher grade levels, this number will show a good variety of lessons within a single subject area. No need to overwhelm editors with more samples. Also keep your lessons simple.

IX. A FINAL WORD ON SAMPLES

Your writing samples must be professional and cleanly formatted. On top, include name, contact information, word count and reading level. Add page numbers, if a sample requires more than one page. For the manuscript itself use a 12-point font, with one inch margins and single spacing, double space between topics or stanzas. Mike and Sandra typically use Times New Roman.

Writing your samples *will take time!* It's important to make these samples top quality. This is what gets your foot in the educational publishing door! However, we do have good news for authors who've written manuscripts that haven't yet been acquired.

Did that sound strange? Here's what we mean. If you have a backlog of unsold manuscripts, you can save time by sifting through those first. You might be able to repurpose unsold manuscripts. Hurrah! Mike did this with a Mosquito manuscript he had written for the Trade Market. It never sold there, and probably never will. But he tweaked it, shortened it, and it's the primary nonfiction manuscript he uses in his educational writing samples.

Do *not* send old manuscripts "as-is." Revise them to make

ALWAYS WAIT

After you completely finish your writing sample, always put it away for *at least a week* without looking at it. *A month* is better! Then edit it one more time before sending.

sure they fit the guidelines we've discussed. If you don't have a personal backlist of unsold manuscripts, then simply start from scratch. Write a few amazing samples and they will be yours forever, ready to send to the next educational publisher you're anxious to work with.

One notable benefit of writing these samples is the fact you'll be improving your craft at the same time! Showcasing your writing skills in 500 words or less is a lot harder than writing a piece without word count limits. Developing this ability to write to a tight word count will also catapult you into the real-life world of an educational writer—who lives, breathes, plans, and gets paid—all based on assigned word count. Like we said earlier, time to embrace your new role as a World Class Word-Count Afficionado! As an initiation, say that three times fast!

The components of your submission package work together to showcase your life experience, your writing talents, your capacity to do research, and your ability to meet deadlines. Each package will be tailored to a particular publisher. Take the time to prepare all your materials carefully.

As the saying goes, you're only as strong as your weakest link.

The good news is that once you develop a great working relationship with a publisher (which might be after completing one assignment), you could begin receiving steady assignments from them! Yay! This means you don't need to send them any more submission packages—EVER!

Invest the time. It's worth it.

CHAPTER 6

STEP-BY-STEP GUIDE TO SUCCESS
ENTER THE EDUCATIONAL MARKET IN ONLY 8 WEEKS

Let's start with a few phrases.
- No pain. No gain.
- The Lord helps those who help themselves.
- With hard work and effort, you can achieve anything.
- The dictionary is the only place where success comes before work.

You're probably figuring out the gist of this. Like any worthwhile endeavor, writing for the Educational Market will take hard work and determination. But if you put in the effort, the odds are *extremely high* that you will meet your goal!

Getting through this chapter will take great effort! It will be challenging, gratifying, intense, invigorating, exhausting, and ultimately exhilarating. And it will only take eight weeks.

Only eight weeks?

Yes. This is where you dig in and start to write! Our step-by-step guide to completing your submission package assumes you have no previous manuscripts ready to go. If you're already a writer who has a backlog of manuscripts, you might breeze through this much more quickly. For most *new* authors, the eight week program is an intense, effective time limit meant to prevent procrastination and forward their careers. It's realistic, but rigorous.

No need to start tapping away on your computer keyboard yet. Take a deep breath, skim through this chapter, and read the rest of the book. Then you can come back and get started. It's okay. That's what we would do.

For those of you who are crazy enough to get started this very second—what the heck! That's okay, too.

Either way, here's your Step-by-Step Guide to Success:

STEP-BY-STEP GUIDE TO SUCCESS
ENTER THE EDUCATIONAL MARKET IN ONLY EIGHT WEEKS!

WEEK 1

Research Educational Publishers (see Chapter 3)

- Choose your favorite educational publisher.
- Choose a book from one of their series that is similar to what you want to write.
  - Note the name of the series and the grade level it's written for.

Start your First Writing Sample #1 (see Chapter 5)

- Choose Nonfiction, Fiction, Poetry, Reader's Theater, etc.
  - Make sure it has a quick, exciting hook, a narrative arc, and a twist at the end. Use exciting active verbs and fun descriptive nouns.
  - Write an entire first draft!
    - Don't go over 500 words (700 if fiction).
    - The first draft doesn't have to be great. It has to be *finished!*

If you chose a Lesson Plan

- Select a topic that showcases your grasp of grade-level curricula, classroom management, and lesson plan elements.
- Write an entire first draft—or adapt a plan you already have.
  - Use headings, bullets, etc. Leave lots of inviting white space.
  - Don't go over 3 pages.

WEEK 2

Write your Query (see Chapter 5)

Write your query for the *specific publisher* you chose.

Write a complete first draft!

Edit your first draft of Writing Sample #1

Start on Writing Sample #2

Use the same rules as with writing sample #1.

WEEK 3

Finish a first draft of writing Sample #2 this week!

Edit Writing Sample #1 and your query

Start on your Resume (see Chapter 5)

This is fun! You get to brag about *you!* It's a nice break from your writing samples.

Finish a first draft of your resume. Yes. Finish it.

WEEK 4

Take two days off. You deserve it!

Edit Writing Sample #1 and #2 and your query.

Find critique partners. You can search local or national groups and organizations.

WEEK 5

Continue editing Writing Sample#1 and #2 and your query

Get critiques for these.

Look at the educational publishers again

Choose two more you would like to query.

Tweak your original query, one for each of these new companies.

Tweak your original resume, one for each of these new companies.

WEEK 6

Take a 2 day break from writing

Rewrite Writing Sample#1 and #2 and your query using whatever suggestions you found valuable from the critiques

WEEK 7

You should now have:

Writing Sample #1 and #2.

Three queries.

Three resumes.

Go *online* to the three educational companies you will be pitching

Make sure you have their current contact information.

Carefully read their submission guidelines.

Make sure your submission package meets all their criteria.

WEEK 8

Do one final edit of Writing Sample #1 and Writing Sample #2

Do one final edit of your queries and resumes

Start submitting!

Reread your query and resume for company #1. Last chance to correct!

Do NOT enter the publisher's email address until ALL documents have been attached. Entering the email address is the very LAST step before sending out your submission package.

Send out your submission package for company #1.

Finish pitching publisher #1 *completely* before starting on publisher #2. Do NOT write all the emails at once. This technique will help prevent foolish errors.

Repeat the process for company #2 and then company #3.

CONGRATULATIONS! You did it!

Simple, isn't it? Ready. Set. Go!

CHAPTER 7

Landing Assignments

Now we wait. This is the hardest part of being a writer in this industry. Nothing ever happens quickly—except—sometimes—when it does.

That last sentence doesn't make much sense without context. Let us explain further.

Generally, educational publishers work on a seasonal schedule. They might put out twenty, fifty, or a few hundred books a couple of times a year. If you contact them when they are soliciting writers, an editor might get back to you the same day. More likely, the editors will be overwhelmed trying to meet obligations for their current season and may not reply to your email at all. Then, months later, they could run across it and offer you a job. Crazy, huh? The other option is that an editor takes a quick look at your submission package and likes it. She might then send a note saying she'll have a project for you in the future. That's what happened to Mike when he queried Rourke Educational Media. It brought him a warm fuzzy feeling to know he was wanted, but then lead to consternation when the project didn't arrive for another couple months!

Sandra had a similar yet different kind of experience—which also doesn't make much sense without context. She received a quick response from an editor at an educational packager, who was expecting to produce a massive curriculum project for a big-name client. Days later, she did reconnect with Sandra but only to inform her they lost the contract. Drats! That ended

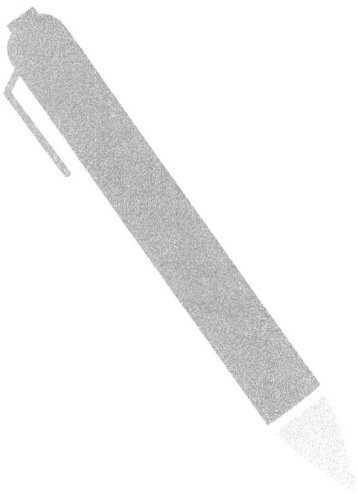

that... until a year later when another editor from a different division reached out on a new project.

Get ready for your own emotional roller coaster now that you've joined the fray.

I. YOU DID IT! YOU DID IT!

Champagne! Noise makers! High fives all around!!

Today your email held a most coveted prize—a note from an editor offering you an educational project. Even better, she offered you TWO books. Hurray! Huzzah!!

Take your time. Dance around the living room. Ruffle the dog's fur. Pet the cat. Hug your spouse. Cheer with the kids. You did it!

Whew! That was fun.

Now it's time to get serious. Pull the email up again and give it a closer look. The first thing you'll notice is that your editor (yes... *your* editor) has asked for a quick reply. Welcome to your first educational deadline. That note is important! You'll want to accept the assignment on the very same day! Why? Because editors need to assign a writer to every book, ASAP. If you delay, those books will be offered to another writer. No lollygagging!

But before you send off your rapid reply, take a moment to consider what the editor actually wrote. She listed the book titles (sometimes a list of books for you to choose from), the word count, book topics, pay, and planned deadlines. Give a close look at the last. That deadline for your first draft is probably within three weeks. Wow! The deadline for final copies of both books is probably within two months, definitely less than three. Oh, my! Make sure you're willing to meet these deadlines. If you are, then type the word, *yes*, and reply to her email.

You're in!

FAST TURNAROUND

If you accept a project during normal business hours, the editor will likely get back to you within 20 minutes. Frequently, even faster!

II. PROJECT OFFER ATTACHMENTS

Basking in the thrill of the moment, there may be a slight niggling in the back of your mind as you consider what you just did. Ignore it for now. Bask a little bit more. Thrill to the joy of becoming a *published* author. You have more information to assimilate, but it can wait a few minutes.

The joy of sending a giddy YES to the editor deserves some time to appreciate.

Ahhhhhhhh.

The next step won't take long. If you accept the editor's offer, she'll send you another email. This one will have two or three attachments: Author's Guidelines, a Contract, and possibly a Manuscript Template. Let's cover the three in a quick overview before dissecting each one.

First, you'll see the *Author's* Guidelines. Don't you love the title? Author's Guidelines. *You* are the author. Enjoy another moment of emotional bliss, then put on your serious face and dig in. This attachment is very important! Okay, all the attachments are very important, but this is your first one.

The Author's Guidelines will list: the titles you'll write, the specs, standards to cover, due dates for outlines and manuscripts, how many sources they expect you to reference, your requirement to write a back cover blurb and metadata description, detailed requirements for word count and sidebars, ATOS level, how to note art specs, what type of glossary, indexes, questions, vocabulary, and activities you'll be expected to write. It might also offer tips or additional notes about the series you are writing for.

WHEW! Take a deep breath. It *does* seem overwhelming, but you can do it. You *will* do it! Remember you already said yes?

Not to worry. We've got this covered. Let's check out the next attachment.

Next is the contract. This will explain very clearly that the publisher has the upper hand in the arrangement. It will state that it is a "Work for Hire" agreement. This means you only get the single total payment they promised for your manuscript, and you will never, ever, no matter what, ever get another penny for it. It restates all your deadlines and the penalties you'll incur if you don't meet them.

If your eyes are bulging out, that's normal.

The final attachment is the manuscript template. It might be sent with this email or possibly forwarded later. This document shows how you'll need to format your manuscript before submitting it. It probably looks like an unintelligible outline with brackets, numbers, and notes.

It's about this moment that your brain recognizes the huge amount of information you've received. It considers the fact you've committed to writing two books in a month and a half—in an unfamiliar format, with questions, glossaries, references, specific reading levels...

Augghhhhh! What have you done? NOW it's time to hyperventilate! Oh! My! GOSH! This is where authors dive into the closet, close the door, and lie in the fetal position. Take some deep breaths while you're in there.

When you finally emerge, we have some good news for you. It's just a phase. Even experienced educational writers go through it. Take another deep breath and slowly let it out. You're not alone. It's an overwhelming amount of information dumped into your email all at once. But, taken one step at a time, you'll do just fine.

Welcome to Educational Publishing!

EDITOR INFO

The editor who contacted you may give you *your* editor's name, email and phone number in an email. If you are working with a book packager, you will be working with two editors, but you will only need to submit to your primary contact.

III. REVIEWING YOUR DOCUMENTS (OUT OF THE CLOSET)

Now that you're back at your computer, we'll explain why there's no need to be overwhelmed like it's a zombie apocalypse. Once you understand the contents of your attachments, it's exhilarating, intellectually stimulating, and even fun!

Let's get started. The first document we'll discuss is the Author Guidelines.

AUTHOR GUIDELINES

Every publisher has their own version of Author Guidelines. This is an overview of how the publisher wants you to interact with them. They will start by giving you your editors name, email, and phone number. In general, contact your editor through email. Later, you might schedule a phone call to do a virtual meet. But only do this after you've thoroughly perused all your documents and can speak intelligibly on your upcoming project.

Your Author's Guidelines will also include:

1. **Titles.**

   A list of the titles you are expected to write.

2. **Specifications (Specs)**

   The specifics of the book. Page count. Word count. Number of sidebars. Captions. Type of art (photos or illustrations). ATOS or Lexile measure.

3. **School Standards**

   Some publishers will indicate the educational standards that are expected to be covered. These might be a version of the Common Core Standards, Next Generation Science Standards (NGSS), or some other listed standard. We'll discuss this topic in detail in Chapter 9 (to be more accurate, *Sandra* will explain it in Chapter 9 while Mike sips some ice cold tea and doodles aimlessly).

   But don't fret about these standards! You won't have to look up any of them. Your publisher will spell out exactly what's needed for any particular section of the book. Simply write the manuscript as assigned, and you'll find you've likely covered the standards already. If not, a few small tweaks while editing can fix any issues.

4. **Deadlines**

   Make careful note here! These are very, very important to the publisher. Look at the deadlines for each of your books; both the outlines, and the final versions. Don't miss them! If for any reason something happens and you might miss one, *immediately, without delay,* tell your editor.

5. **Outline and final manuscript requirements**

   This section gives specifics on what must be included in the outline and manuscript. It might discuss wordcount, content, and number of sidebars. It could list topics to be included in the manuscript. It will spell out require-ments for glossaries, vocabulary words, and backmatter. This is the meat of what you'll be required to write.

6. **References**

   Each publisher has its own requirements for footnotes

and references. They might suggest certain types of bibliography formatting, but the truth is, they really don't care much about the format. *Don't waste your time* trying to make thesis ready footnotes or bibliographies. They simply want to confirm any information you send. In fact, Mike generally includes the link for any online source, nothing else. For books or magazines, he lists the basic information but doesn't fret over formatting. While Sandra considered dragging out her dog-eared copy of *The Chicago Manual of Style,* and trying out research software, like Scrivener or Zotero, thank goodness she discovered from her editor that nothing formal was needed. Like Mike, she keeps a simple list of links for online sources, though she may take an occasional screen shot for her own records. For books and magazines, she records basic details, with no worries about proper formatting.

Most importantly, you must have *reliable* sources to document. We'll discuss this in more detail when we cover the research phase of writing your manuscript.

7. Additional Information
The guidelines will also note additional requirements. This could be anything from providing an author photo and bio to defining what type of grade level measuring system to use, to specifying how to describe your art requests.

8. Guidelines for Large Curriculum Projects
Many curriculum projects like lesson plans or teacher guides include basic specifications, standards, deadlines, and even references and source listings. However, there are some differences in the massive, fast-moving curriculum projects you may be working on with teams of others. These projects often include detailed style guides for everything—terms, quantities of sidebars, when to use bulleted lists, and more. Also, you're given large spreadsheets that list everything—all the projects, the standards, the lesson objectives, and more. This is so you understand how your assignments fit into the larger program. You're also asked to join temporary platforms that will enable you to pick up and deposit your completed materials, communicate with your editor or

others on your team instantly, or gain access to instructional materials you may need to create your product. While this may seem daunting, everything soon falls into place and runs like a well-oiled machine. Your editor is always eager to help.

IV. THE CONTRACT

An educational publisher's contract is an interesting creature. It's both vitally important, and of little use to read; except to make sure the book titles, deadlines, and pay schedules are listed properly.

Why? Because in today's environment, the publisher has the upper hand.

Their contract protects them, not you. It will start by listing the books you agreed to write, and immediately tell you that the publisher will own *all* the rights to your books. It gives deadlines for each title, followed by the financial penalties (a reduction in your pay) you'll incur if you don't meet them. It spells out your pay and when to expect it in your bank account or in the mail. Another important note is that the publisher can, *at any time,* modify your work. This is even after your final submission is complete and payment has been received.

The contract will also note how many author copies you will get—typically two. Mike tried several times to increase the number of author copies, but *never* with any success. As a consolation prize, sometimes the publisher will have a reduced rate for authors if they want to buy additional copies. If you're writing curriculum materials, especially if they're within a larger curriculum program, it's not likely that you'll get any copies. You may wish to save your original manuscript in a folder on your computer, although this isn't always practical. Also, it may go against a confidentiality or nondisclosure agreement you've signed.

The rest of the contract is typical lawyer-speak that works to the benefit of the publisher, covering quality of work, revisions,

CONTRACT CONCERNS

Signing your first contract may trigger some anxiety! Rest assured when you sign your second, third, or fourth—the feeling will pass.

confidentiality, legal jurisdiction in the event of conflict, and other such topics.

The point being—you have given up *all rights* after your manuscript is officially submitted. Before we move on to the more pleasant aspects of the Educational Market, let's talk about one of your primary concerns—pay.

The contract gives the publisher the copyright to any manuscript you submit. This is called "work-for-hire." You get one pre-determined amount of pay for each submission. Since these publishers deal with hundreds of books per year, they have a standard amount of pay they assign to each book, typically based upon word length. This amount varies greatly between publishers! For a 500 word manuscript, this pay could range from $250 to $2500. It's typically at the lower end of that scale, less than $750. This is the total amount you'll get for your manuscript. You'll never receive another penny for your efforts, regardless of how well your book sells. If you're a reliable repeat writer, it's possible you could get this amount *slightly* increased, but probably not, and almost never as a newbie.

Why do they force this less than equitable contract on writers? Educational publishers will say that many of their books go quickly out of print due to the timeliness of their topics and the fact that many use photos (which can quickly date a book). Also, in the past they sold almost exclusively to schools and libraries where future sales weren't a significant source of income.

These excuses have since grown flimsy. Today, your educational book will appear on Amazon and other book sites soon after its release date. It will be available in both print-on-demand hardcopy as well as eBook formats. This means your manuscript will be in stock forever, with never an additional cent finding its way back to you.

That's the environment today. If you want to write for this market, you'll sign their contract, perhaps with a wistful sigh. The odds are you won't be able to make any changes.

As a note of interest, the Trade Market and Educational Market continue to overlap, even more than in the past. The distinction between the two can blur in many cases. Some Trade publishers acquire and print books that have many Educational Market characteristics, yet they pay royalty based rates. In return, Educational publishers acquire books more suited to the Trade Market, but still pay a one time "work-for-hire" rate. Not what us authors want! Some Educational publishers have a small segment of books they acquire with royalty pay rates, but it's difficult to submit to this sector without an agent.

Another element included in contracts for traditional Educational Market projects *and* curriculum projects is a nondisclosure clause. This is a statement you must agree to that prevents you from discussing or sharing details about your assignment with anyone. Publishers work hard to protect their ideas, their products, and their ability to be first-to-market. So no social media posts announcing your new assignment! This isn't often a problem once the book is off press. After you receive your copy, feel free to hit the social media circuit and claim your bragging rights. Yet be aware that even then, you may need to reign in your bragging rights based on the agreements you've signed, though we have never found this to be an issue.

For educators, the packagers that produce massive curriculum projects for well-known educational publishers try to keep a low profile. Their publisher clients might not want the general public to know they didn't create their own product inhouse.

The bottom line? Most current Educational Market contracts are "work-for-hire," one-sided, in favor of the publisher. But, don't feel cheated. If you're trying to break into the writing business, it's one way to improve your skills while getting paid to do so.

Not a bad deal!

V. MANUSCRIPT TEMPLATE

The final attachment you'll get is exactly as the title implies— a template for writing your manuscript. This is the format the publisher wants you to use for your final manuscript submission. With so many books to publish at once, it's easier for editors to peruse a standardized format, with a place for everything and everything in its place.

As a new educational writer, the template can be confusing. Don't worry! The template has simple directions included throughout. You'll probably figure it out on your own. If there's anything you're not sure about, simply list your questions and email them to your editor. Or call your editor and ask! It's not a problem. That's what editors do.

Mike did a horrible job for his first couple of books as he tried to figure out the template. His editor was not overly impressed, but she was professional and helpful, giving positive suggestions and tips. Her reward was that Mike became a seasoned educational writer, greatly reducing her workload in the future!

Fortunately, everything gets easier after you've done it once.

Each follow-on book with the same publisher will flow more smoothly, since you'll understand exactly what the editor needs.

Any large curriculum projects you take on will also use templates. These are like ones you might use with traditional educational market books, except the formatted content is suited to lesson plans. These, too, may be confusing at first. They can be so large that a separate style booklet is included in your guidelines so you can complete it correctly. Yet after one or two, they become routine. Sandra has worked on some big projects where the style guide was created as her team completed templates. While this can be frustrating, it is also the nature of some of these massive projects. Not every detail is known before a team begins work. The schedules are just too tight to await perfection. Editors may have to swing back and adjust. It's all part of the process.

VI. READY. SET. GO!

The instant you're no longer giddy with delight or paralyzed with fear, it's time to move! This doesn't mean putting pen to paper...not yet. Your first steps involve setting up *offline* research—any source of information you might use that isn't instantly accessible online. This important step needs to be taken *immediately* because the lead time for gathering information offline can take a couple of weeks, which eats up a significant part of your deadline!

Offline research includes things like:
- Searching your library for books and ordering them ASAP.
    - Look for any books or magazines related to your subject.
    - Look for similar series from other educational publishers.
- Lining up experts for testimonials or quotes if you plan to use them.
    - Send out a carefully worded email asking for their assistance ASAP (samples in the addendum)
- Planning a trip to nearby facilities with pertinent information
    - Mike lives near Cape Canaveral which has wonderful information on space related topics.
    - Museums, nature centers, wildlife preserves, or any facility related to your topic can get the creative juices flowing and make your manuscript a standout.

That's it! Easy, huh? Now take the next few days to peruse your paperwork, get familiar with it, and develop a plan of attack for actually *writing* your project.

Yes. You have a little time to breath, brag, daydream, and rest up for the frantic days ahead. Enjoy!

TEMPORARY EXPERT

The term, coined by educational writer extraordinaire, Paula Morrow, is spot on! You'll become a temporary expert on the topic you're assigned.

CHAPTER 8

RESEARCH. RESEARCH. RESEARCH.

A.B.O.D + 4.

ABOD—you ask? *Obviously,* it means Actual Book Offer Day + 4.

Okay. Mike made up that acronym even though he doesn't like acronyms! Sandra didn't have the strength to argue anymore, so it's stuck in the book. Feel free to look the other way and move on.

The important thing is to highlight the time frame we're working with—it's about four days after receiving your assignment, 5:30 am. The house is quiet. You have a mug of coffee steaming beside you. You're set up for a successful morning of writing. Where do you start?

If it's a topic you're intimately familiar with, you'll start with an outline. Have the Author's Guidelines readily available, pull up the manuscript template, and start writing! How cool would that be if your first book was actually on a topic you knew something about!

Score!

More likely, because you are a new author, you were offered the titles that no one else took. You had a choice of two: How Rocket Engines Work, and The Social Life of Lemmings.

At this moment, you're thrilled you only took one of the titles, not both. But your knowledge of rocket engines is still sorely lacking.

Since you're writing on a topic you know nothing about, you'll start your morning with some online research.

I. RESEARCHING YOUR TOPIC

In today's world, most research is done online. That's both good and bad. Good, because you can do it from the comfort of your home. Bad, because the online world is glutted with false information, urban legends, mom myths, misunderstandings, and plenty of outright lies.

Fortunately, a careful researcher can navigate through this mass of misinformation and uncover legitimate sites that have actual facts, empirical data, and valid findings.

How? Let's start by covering what *NOT* to do.

Things You Should *NEVER* Do when Researching Online
1. Never use social media as a source.
    a. Facebook, Instagram, X (formerly Twitter), and other social media are hotbeds of misinformation. They promote opinions, not facts.
2. Don't simply google and pull information from the first page that loads.
    a. Hits on google can be ads or websites with non-validated information
3. Don't use Wikipedia as a source
    a. Wikipedia is a great place to find references you can use, but it's not a valid, verified source

Now let's look at what you CAN do to find good information on the internet.

Things You Should *ALWAYS* Do when Researching Online
1. Use authoritative websites
    a. If you're researching a medical book, use sites like the CDC, Mayo clinic, or Harvard medical. For history you can use museum websites like the Smithsonian, the Louvre, or the British Museum. For space research, NASA or the European Space Agency would be a couple of good choices. Always check to make sure you're on the correct website and not a scam website.

2. Find original documentation
    a. If you're referencing data from a study, then find the original documentation for that study. It might be at the National Library of Medicine or National Institute of Health. Don't use someone else's reference. Museum sites are terrific for having pictures of original historical documents. The Library of Congress is another incredible resource where you can search for original documents. Do you need a map of Ft. Pickens drawn during the Civil War? Original newspaper articles on the Spanish Flu? This is the place to search.

THE PACIFIC NORTHWEST TREE OCTOPUS?

Another hoax, this example is used in school classrooms everywhere to teach students about the misleading nature of many internet websites. Check it out!

One excellent example of misleading information on the internet is the Hundredth Monkey Phenomena. This refers to an account of monkeys on an isolated island in Japan who taught themselves to wash the sand off sweet potatoes. Once the "hundredth monkey" had learned the habit, monkeys from other isolated islands spontaneously picked up the habit. Or so the rumor spread. This led to the "New Age" belief that when enough people join in the same consciousness, they can cause change in others.

Is it true?

Mike heard the story from a friend who showed him several articles from different magazines supporting the belief. His friend purported it must absolutely be true because it could be found in a variety of sources. How would you research this?

1. Read the articles
    a. Upon reading the articles, it was obvious the information had all come from the same source. The articles stated the information had "been verified" or "was taken from a scientific study" but none referenced the exact study.
2. Track down the origin
    a. Although Wikipedia is NOT a reference to use, it can *lead* you to some good references.
    b. Lyall Watson (a New Age author) first told the anecdote in his book Lifetide (1979). In this book he purported the phenomena and referenced a

scientific study of monkeys by Masao Kawai (and others) done circa 1965 in Japan.

    c. An interesting note here is that Lyall Watson did reference a real scientific study. Had anyone bothered to investigate further, they would have noted that *the study proved Watson's statements to be false.*

3. Find a highly respected source that discusses the subject.

    a. The Skeptical Inquirer is *The Gold Standard* of research on questionable claims. They are happy to prove claims either true or false based on the facts.

    b. In 1985 the Skeptical Inquirer (author Ron Amundson) published a clear and concise article explaining how the "Hundredth Monkey" effect had always been a false claim.

4. Find a copy of the original study

    a. With a little tenacity you can find photos of the original study and documentation (English translation) from 1965. You can now draw your own conclusion.

This is the perfect example of how you, as a writer, must do careful research to get at the facts. The "prevailing truth" and the most popular google responses are not always true.

The more online research you do, the more you'll notice how authoritative websites and scam websites differ. You'll also find that many different sites reference a single article, whether or not it's true.

It's up to you to dig out the truth.

Sometimes, no matter how hard you try, you might find conflicting information on a topic. What do you do in that case? Call your editor, discuss the problem, and the two of you will arrive at a solution.

In the educational writing business, editors want to know immediately about any problems, concerns, delays, or questions. Since *they* are on a deadline too, quick action to diffuse any problems goes a long way toward developing a successful relationship.

II. USING EXPERTS

It may seem overwhelming to find and speak to experts on a given topic, but there's no need to hyperventilate. It's possible you'll *never* need an expert's opinion. Mike has *never* contacted a single expert in *any* of his educational writing. Ever!

Oops! Not so fast!! That statement was true until the month before this book went to print! That's when he signed on with Redline to do two books—one about becoming an Aircraft Mechanic and another about becoming a Respiratory Therapist. Both required expert knowledge and quotes.

Library and online research provide more than enough information for most educational projects.

Fortunately, if you do need an expert, it's a straightforward process.

REQUEST FOR EXPERTS SAMPLES

Samples appear in the Appendix. '

1. Search the internet for experts.
2. Find the expert you're interested in talking to (college and university staff seem to be especially helpful).
3. Send an email introduction with your request.

Most of them are thrilled to help!

Mike had previously used experts for a couple of his Trade books. One example is a book he wrote about Otto Lilienthal. He contacted the Lilienthal Museum in Germany and ended up interacting with two museum directors. They were both thrilled to help.

Subject matter experts are experts because they *love* their subject matter! They *want* to get the correct facts out.

Sandra had to include statements from industry experts in her book on dance careers. Not having a lot of contacts in the field, she reached out to a former student who played a lead role in many of her school district's high school musicals. Crazy, right! At the time she was working on the dance book, he was a "struggling actor" trying to launch his career in New York City.

His list of industry contacts was big, and his insights of "Whose-Who" in the performing arts industry was current. He eagerly shared both with Sandra. With this start and her own online research, she was able to choose and contact a rich variety of dancers, choreographers, physical therapists, agents, set designers, and others. She recorded her conversations, pulled out great statements to include in the book, and even secured head shots to feature with the statements. All, with only a small amount of hyperventilating!

If you're planning to quote industry experts or use their statements in a book, make sure to get signed release forms. These are provided by the publisher. You should also make note of their assistance in the acknowledgements page or elsewhere in your book, if this option is available to you.

CHAPTER 9

Writing Your Manuscript

You're in the club! You're an actual author now, with a real live editor. That's a great step in the right direction for your writing career. To keep things on track, there are a few things to know about this new author/editor relationship.

First, your editor is very, very busy. She has many authors to work with and many, many books. Nor is she only working on these projects. She still has to consider upcoming seasons and also tie up any loose ends from previous work. She doesn't have a lot of spare time.

Translated, this means most of your interactions will be via email. It will give her time to digest what you need and to reply to your requests when she has the time. Most editors get back to email queries very quickly, almost always on the same day if not within the hour.

However, if there's a topic that requires some discussion or if you're unsure of something, you absolutely should call your editor on the phone. She'll be happy to talk and explain away any uncertainties. To show your professionalism it's best to email for a convenient time to chat for both of you.

Percentage wise, maybe 90% of interactions will be email, 10% phone.

I. THE MANUSCRIPT OUTLINE

One thing you'll find with every project is that you need to submit an outline. Sometimes the directions are very specific as to content, other times not. Refer to your Author Guidelines for the proper format.

An interesting conundrum with the outline is that you may find yourself writing an outline with the same word count as your book! It seems crazy to do so. However, that's what editors want. They want to see how you plan to lay out the book with your ideas.

But wait, you might ask. Why not simply write the full manuscript if it's one of those with a word count of about a thousand or less? Why bother with an outline? You can simply finish the manuscript and make changes to that.

Great idea? No. In fact, it's a VERY BAD idea! How do we know? Because Mike tested out that very technique. And since he's not always a quick learner, he tried it twice. The result? Two full rewrites with many changes after that. Yuck.

Editors want an outline because they want to tweak the tone and content before you start the manuscript. They need to match *your* outline with those of the authors writing other books in the series. They need continuity through each series they create.

Sandra's approach to outlining was smarter (oops...I meant to say "different") than Mike's. For example, in her book on dance careers, she had to fit many different careers into a 1500 word 32-page book. She used the outlining process to help her make decisions about the organization and the depth and scope of the content for each career prior to writing. Another time, she had to create an outline for the first book in a ten-volume study series for students in grades 6–8 on the Language Arts standards. In addition to outlining the skills in the first volume, she was intent on determining if the outline would "hold up" and work well for all the other volumes which covered different skills. It turned out to be a good exercise because the outline wasn't a good fit for the project as a whole and she changed it before submitting a better one to the publisher.

CRAFTING OUTLINES

Your outline not only shows an editor the content you intend to include—and possibly exclude—but it also features your take or spin on the topic.

Editors need this overview of what the book will look like before they commit to your plan. They'll always have some changes to how they want the book to flow or where they want information presented. It's much easier to iron these out in the outline rather than have full rewrites of your work. Your best bet is to make the outlining process work for you...as well as the publisher.

II. ON TO THE STORY

With the outline complete you'll have a much better idea of what your final product will look like. You'll know what your editor wants and she'll give direction where she thinks you need it. Now it's time for the manuscript itself!

In this section, we'll talk about the different facets of your manuscript; from "leveling" your work, to writing snappy side bars, to everything in-between. Always reference your Author Guidelines to make sure you're staying on track.

III. ATOS, LEXILE, AND LEVELING

Let's start with leveling. Remember a couple months ago when you sent in your wonderful submissions package? On it you said, "I'm comfortable writing at different grade levels." What you really meant to say was that you knew big kids used big words and little kids used little words.

Uh, oh.

Don't worry. It's not a problem. Leveling is a simple concept you'll quickly become comfortable with. Leveling a book means writing it for a particular grade level, or more accurately, a particular reading level. It really is almost as simple as "small kids = small words, big kids = big words" concept.

To write at a lower reading level, use short, easy-to-understand words, short sentences, and repeat words. *Goodnight Moon* has a very low reading level. It uses simple words, short sentences, and repeats words over and over. To write at a higher level, do the opposite. Use a higher vocabulary, longer sentences, and don't repeat words as much. Simple.

In kids' book writing, the problem is almost always getting the reading level lower. To simplify this, we've included a quick guide below to help you out.

HOW TO LOWER THE READING LEVEL
1. Vocabulary
    a. Use short, simple words.
    b. Use age-appropriate words. If you're not sure what's appropriate for a given age, do a quick online search to find the answer.
    c. Repeat words.
    d. Use fewer proper nouns.
    e. Try not to use technical jargon or specialty vocabulary.
2. Sentences
    a. Use short, simple sentences. If a sentence becomes too long, divide it in half.
    b. Don't use too much punctuation. Fewer commas, quotes, colons, etc. means a lower reading level.
    c. Use simple subheadings in nonfiction.
3. Characters and Plot
    a. Use fewer characters.
    b. Use chronological order—no flashbacks or alternate viewpoints.
    c. Use simple concepts. Less abstract is better.

TECHNICAL JARGON

No matter how simple you keep the reading level, most projects include technical terms. Using these terms in the manuscript will raise the ATOS or Lexile level. Your editor understands this. Your ATOS level will frequently be slightly higher than they suggested in the guidelines.

Now that you know *how* to take your story to a lower level, how do you know what level you are supposed to write at? The answer will be clearly stated in your writer's guidelines. That's where you'll first see a reference to an ATOS or Lexile measure. Let's take a moment to cover those.

ATOS and Lexile are two separate programs that can analyze text and determine what the reading level is. Your publisher will sometimes provide a link for one of these, noted in their Author Guidelines, along with the level you should be writing at. After you've written a part of your manuscript, you simply input your text for an ATOS or Lexile analysis.

As of today, you can still go online, search for "ATOS analyzer," and access the analyzer for free. It has gone back and forth from being a free service to a paid service.

ATOS will give a readability level like 4.2, meaning the text would be appropriate for readers in the 2nd month of the fourth grade. A level of 3.6 would be a reading level appropriate to third graders in their 6th month of school.

A Lexile measure will give you a number from below 0 up to 1600. For numbers below zero you'll see something like BR50. BR means beginning reader. You'll likely be working in the positive 200-800 range. What does that mean? Simply go online and pull up a Lexile table or use the one your publisher sent. It takes the Lexile score and references it to a reading level range. A 350-450 Lexile score, or 350L-450L, equates to about a 1st-2nd grade reading level.

You'll quickly find out that it's easy and tempting to write at a higher level than the publisher wants.

Meaning, you'll constantly be trying to lower the level of your manuscript. Take this into account as you write, to prevent excessive editing later. Use short words, short sentences, and simple vocabulary. If you find yourself using run on sentences, simply put a period somewhere and start a new sentence.

If you're unsure of what type of vocabulary to use, find a few books your publisher has (in the same grade level) and get a feel for words they use. You can also do online searches for grade level vocabulary. Sandra uses an online source occasionally, if she questions a specific word when creating test questions. Curriculum publishers often make an online source available for writers to use for this purpose. Finally, there are references, like the *Children's Writer's Word Book,* that list words and their associated grade level. Neither one of us use this type of dictionary, but for those who prefer to see the list in black and white, it might be helpful.

IV. SNEAKY SIDEBARS

Hurrah for sidebars! We LOVE sidebars! Sidebars are the best!! Sidebars are a wonderfully delectable, extraordinarily useful part of educational publishing. They give authors the opportunity to provide tasty tidbits of information while simultaneously solving issues with reading level and topic coverage. Plus, they're just plain cool. We LOVE sidebars!

Let's look at how sidebars manage to sneak in and solve a couple of issues you might have with your manuscript.

We've already discussed how manuscripts need to be written at a particular reading level. Sometimes this is difficult. It's not easy to get complex information across in a level and tone that a young reader can understand.

Viola! Enter the sidebar. The text in a sidebar doesn't need to meet the leveling criteria of the manuscript at large. You still need to provide clear explanations and simple, concise information, but when the editor checks your manuscript for reading level, she doesn't include the sidebars. This allows sidebars to contain a few more scientific terms or a bit more complex information without increasing the reading level of the manuscript as a whole.

Then there's the bonus of increased topic coverage. As you might imagine, writing a 1,000 word (or less) manuscript about satellites in space, computer coding, or the finer points of insect mating, can be challenging. You don't have many words to cover the topic. You'll probably discover you can't fit all the information you want into your manuscript. Sidebars help address the problem. A topic you can't fit in can be referenced in a sidebar. It won't have to fit into your primary storyline. Fascinating information related to your topic can thus be covered in a separate, succinct, note. How cool is that!

Depending on your manuscript, you'll write sidebars as strictly text, or as text with a photo. The text *only* sidebars are self-explanatory, but *sidebars with photos* require a special writing technique.

Let's take a look.

THE ART OF THE SIDEBAR

Who knew of their subtle superbness! It's no wonder you might feel intimidated writing them. Rest assured this is but another skill you'll master with time.

If our sidebar is a picture of a lion in the jungle, we wouldn't put text in that says, "A lion in the jungle." With photo sidebars, we use the opportunity to add interesting tidbits of information. We might say something like, "Lions are the only cats that live in groups, called prides," or "Male lions can weigh nearly 500 pounds." That way we've added value to the photo and knowledge to our young readers.

A lion in the jungle.

Lions are the only cats that live in groups, called prides.

Male lions can weigh nearly 500 pounds.

A stage with
colorful lighting.

Creative new lighting
blends high tech and
the arts.

   Another example would be a performance stage with
colorful overhead and floor lighting. If the sidebar is a picture
of a stage with colorful lighting, we would not subtitle it "A
stage with colorful lighting." Instead, we might say, "Creative
new lighting blends high tech and the arts." This caption
serves its dual purpose well.

V. TEMPTING TITLES

After perusing a couple of educational books, you'll discover they are broken into bite size chunks of information. Instead of being written as long-winded essays, they're divided into segments easily digestible by young readers. This provides you with a wonderful opportunity to invent inviting, juicy, or captivating chapter titles and subtitles. Writing fun-filled unique titles is a great place to showcase your skills and increase reader excitement! For example, let's say you're writing about SETI. Instead of titling the chapter *SETI—the Search for Extra-terrestrial Intelligence* you'd write something like *Calling All Aliens.* Information about SETI would be explained within the text or in a sidebar. If you were writing about Mt. Everest, you wouldn't title the chapter *Climbing a Mountain.* No thrill in that! Instead your title might be *Standing on Top of the World,* a title sure to spark a young reader's interest. If your topic is about symbiotic relationships, you might title the section *Weird & Wacky Pairs in the Wild,* which is an actual work-in-progress that Mike and Sandra have *paired up* to write! Think about terrible puns like this your parents have made over the years. Now it's your turn!

See how fun this is? Use your imagination! Your manuscript will stand out with its wily wit, silly puns, and curious comments that lure readers into every chapter.

VI. HOOK AND TONE

Every book needs a hook—some fascinating fact, twist of a phrase, or knowledge tickling tidbit that pulls a reader in from the moment she picks up the book. This can be more difficult to do in the Educational Market because there are very strict limits on the format, structure, and tone of a book depending on the publisher and series you are writing for. This is especially true in the photo-illustrated nonfiction type of series.

Mike ran into this problem when he first started writing for the Educational Market. His initial hook, written with playful style and witty wordplay, did not fit well into the more staid and structured writing style of the series he was adding too. He still thinks of this as the "pizza parlor incident," since the scene began in a pizza parlor to introduce a book on gluten. Demerits for Mike because he didn't do enough research on that publisher's similar books before he started writing. Double demerits because he thought his writing was so witty that it would work in this particular manuscript. That is NEVER the case. Educational publishers typically have several writers for each series and they want the series to be consistent!

Your job as a writer is to bring your polished writing style and fit it within the confines of your assigned series.

Which brings us back to the hook.

Even with strict guidelines, you can still find plenty of interesting information and twists of words that will hook a reader and have them begging to read more. Simply make sure your amazing information aligns with the tone of the series. Don't skimp on this important introduction to *your* book! It will set a precedent for the book and for future writing assignments.

In contrast, if you are fortunate enough to land a *fiction* project with an educational publisher, you'll be able to use every nuanced twist of phrase and alliterative allegory you desire. Your kid-friendly introduction will smoothly flow from pen to paper or fingertips to keyboard. These fiction projects tend to be less formally structured—*in general*—except for word count, reading level, and series continuity.

It's all part of adjusting your writing style to mesh with the publisher's needs.

VII. DOCUMENT EVERYTHING IMMEDIATELY!

Yes, we touched on research earlier and warned you that a deeper dive was ahead. Here it is! In nonfiction, research is a fundamental, integral, incredibly significant part of every manuscript. It is *very* important to the publisher to be able to check your references and make sure they're valid. It is very important to *you* because you'll be searching the internet for hours as you gather information. Everything will become a blur.

The lesson we want to pass along? When doing research DOCUMENT EVERYTHING IMMEDIATELY! Not one minute later, or one hour later, or tomorrow. Now. NOW. NOW!

Whew! Sorry about the explosion, but you'll be in a much better place if you take this advice to heart.

When researching a nonfiction project, you'll probably do most of it online, although it's great if you have books, magazines, or subject matter experts you can also reference. But the type of research you're doing isn't what we're focused on here. We're focused on the problems you'll run into if you don't document as you go along.

Here's a typical scenario. You're doing research on planets in our solar system. You have six different websites open, from NASA to scientific journals, to the Air and Space Museum. You might even have a magazine or book you're referencing. You've hit your groove and it's one of those magical moments when the writing comes easily and you're whizzing along one paragraph after another, You click back and forth through the websites, flip through your magazine, and add one amazing anecdote after another to your manuscript. It's terrific. It's magical. It's wonderful!

Until...

Until you slow down and decide to add the references. Where did that cool note about the temperature of Venus come from? Where did you learn that Saturn's largest moon, Titan, rains ethane and methane instead of water?

Oops. Time to track down those references you ignored earlier. This laborious process can take longer than it took to write your manuscript. This is what we do NOT want to happen.

Instead, document as you go. This doesn't mean you have to perfectly format your documentation each time you use a new tidbit of data. Not at all. It simply means you need to jot down, or somehow document, *where* you got information the instant you decide to use it in your manuscript.

FOOTNOTE

The footnote feature is one way to keep track of your research. The moment you find a great website, make a note of its content and copy the web address to a footnote. You'll be glad you did!

You'll want to find the reference immediately when you note it later in your manuscript.

How can you best do this? Like most things, it depends on your personality and how you've developed your writing skills over the years.

Mike has a notable weakness in the "proper skills of documentation." His formal education was sadly lacking in that category—or perhaps he slept through those classes. Either way, Mike learned a hard lesson with his first couple of nonfiction projects. He wrote the manuscripts without immediately documenting his information, and it cost him hours of post-writing reference-searching to find his sources again. Some he was never able to find!

To preclude that from ever happening again, when using an online source, he takes a screen shot of every page that he might reference later. He also copies the link and places it alongside the text he just wrote. Two layers of safety! He does a similar thing with books or magazines, taking a photo of the book and page with the source information. He also keeps a word document list where he jots down quick notes on where he is using the various sources. This may seem a bit cumbersome, but it's what works for him.

Sandra's system is similar. For online research, she copies and inserts links as comments in the margin of a "working text". This makes it easy to compile a list of them, which is what most publishers want. She duplicates her working text, removes the comments, and ends up with a clean, submittable manuscript to insert into the publisher's template. Easy-Peasy!

Like Mike, Sandra also takes screen shots and files them with her working text, especially if the information refutes common beliefs or is surprising and may raise an editors' eyebrows! In other words, she anticipates and prepares for editor questions and delivers a double whammy of support – an online citation and a screen shot of the reference. BAM! BAM! And of course, she ensures that all her sites are reputable from the get-go.

Books, scholarly journals, and other hardcopy materials are a different story. She keeps a Google Doc list for each project and records key details on her resources there. Although there are numerous writer/research software programs like Scrivner, Zotero, End Note, Dabble, ProWritingAid, and countless others—which many of Sandra's writer friends and academic research colleagues use—Sandra likes her simple and reliable If-It-Ain't-Broke system.

As you're probably figuring out, there are an infinite variety of ways to keep track of sources as you're penning your manuscript. The one thing they all have in common is to do it IMMEDIATELY. Do NOT wait until later. If you follow this rule, then any system that works for you should be just fine.

VIII. ACCURACY IS THE KEY TO SUCCESS

Now that we've covered the importance of immediate documentation, it's time to consider how this research is written into your manuscript. First and foremost, be accurate! You took a big step toward accuracy when you made sure to use only the highest quality websites and most authoritative sources. The second half of the accuracy process is considering how you write this information you learned into your manuscript.

Let's say you are writing about half a glass of water. Depending on your mood, you might write that the glass is half full or the glass is half empty. Great! No problem. Both of those statements are true. But let's change it up a bit.

Let's say the glass of water is now slightly more than half full. Just a little bit more. Since it's so close to half full can you simply fudge a bit and say, "the glass is half full?" The answer is no! That's not an accurate statement. You know it's not true. Instead, you can say the glass is *about* half full or *close to* half full or *approximately* half full. All of these statements are 100% accurate. Using these types of modifying words are an important part of writing nonfiction for the Educational Market.

Using our previous example of researching outer space, let's say you want to write about the distance of the moon from the earth. You'll quickly discover the moon has an elliptical orbit. It orbits from nearly 252,000 miles away, to as close as 225,623 miles away with an average distance of about 239,000 miles.

Let's dissect this last paragraph. It's an example of how to write accurate statements for your nonfiction manuscript. First, I used a valid, authoritative source for my information. Then, I used modifiers when necessary. For example, I said the moon *orbits nearly 252,000 miles away.* I said *nearly* 252,000 because the actual distance I found was 252,088 miles, but I didn't want to confuse the issue with too many numbers. I took an opposite approach on my next statement, saying the moon *could be as close as 225,623 miles.* In this case I used the exact number from an authoritative source, so I didn't use any modifying words like *about* 225,623 miles or *nearly* 225,623 miles. Finally, I summed it up by saying the moon was an average distance of *about 239,000* miles. This ensured that my statement, and my writing, was completely accurate.

Although it may seem silly or trite to emphasize these types of statements, it is an important facet of nonfiction writing.

We don't ever want to make definitive statements that aren't actually true.

Your editor would be unhappy if she found out, and most important, we don't want to write books that are inaccurate or misleading to our young readers.

Is there a limit to this? Absolutely. Depending on the grade level you're writing for, you might approximate or round numbers differently. The younger the reader, the simpler your numbers should be.

You'll also need to be careful when you're quoting or summarizing a subject. If you're using an actual quote, make sure it's accurate and unchanged. No throwing in extra words or switching them around to make the quote sound better. If you're summarizing a statement, make sure your summary follows the true intent of the speaker or writer you've taken the information from.

Finally, a last trap that's easy to fall into is taking something for granted because you've heard it your entire life and believe it to be true. Perhaps it's a belief held by your parents, family, or friends that you've grown up with. This is particularly noticeable in today's social media, where blatant untruths are frequently accepted as fact with no basis in reality.

An interesting anecdote to this is that Mike grew up driving barefoot, and continues to do so to this day. Over the course of time, several people told him it was illegal, but it wasn't until a friend hounded him for this "illegal habit" that he finally looked it up. Using proper research protocol, he went directly to an authoritative website, the state DMV website. Interestingly, the website included a note saying that many people believed driving barefoot was illegal! It then stated that this was *not* the case. There was no law or restriction of any sort against driving barefoot.

The moral to the story is that just because you *believe* something is true, doesn't make it true! You need to determine with 100% certainty it is true, before making any claims in your manuscript.

IX. SENSITIVE CONTENT

Just as you must bring a titanic-size amount of professionalism to your research, the same is true for your treatment of sensitive content. You don't want a burgeoning writing career to capsize before it even gets started!

Educational publishers must exercise care *and* caution over sensitive content. "Sensitive" could mean anything that their market—teachers, librarians, administrators, parents, schools, and students who inhabit them—perceives as sensitive.

That's a lot of perceivers!

Political, religious, historic, and timely social issues are some of the broad topics within this category. These ticking timebombs can clear out a large family dinner well before Uncle Mort's rhubarb pie is served! Your job is not to express personal views, but rather to present your painstaking research while keeping all biases in check.

This means your biography on a high-profile political figure, your nonfiction book on little-known religious customs, and your factual account of an historical event are *not* to contain even a smidgeon of personal remark—dissent, approval, or judgement. Stick to the facts. Your writing should be objective and disciplined.

You can always decline a project or steer clear of publishers who flock to these topics if you're not comfortable with the content.

If you have any questions—or if you're getting tossed in the tides of second guessing, run your ideas by your editor. He'll be happy to help at an early stage, which beats having to inform you three weeks into the deadline that your outline must be reworked—a lot!

This kind of sensitive content is *usually* reserved for grades 6 and above (the scope of this book is primarily K–5), yet this is shifting quickly. Your publisher routinely solicits feedback from librarians, teachers, and others on their wants and needs, their like and dislikes, and any challenges or successes they've faced with the publishers' books. Armed with this helpful information, your editor can steer you in the right direction.

This issue is significant because a lack of sensitivity can result in complications in the classroom.

Imagine you're a new teacher pushing open the door to your school's vast bookroom for the very first time. It contains class-size sets of roughly 20 copies of the same book. The section you're interested in is for grades 3 and 4. Wait! Did you say 20 copies? Yes. If your book is picked up by teachers for classroom instruction, a 20-unit purchase is typical. (Not that you'll get any more money, but you will have earned some fame and your editor's unwavering admiration! Woo-hoo! Pat on the back for you!) But back to our bookroom... Your heart pounds with excitement. Your hands twitch, eagerly preparing to pull bins from the shelves. When suddenly, you're distracted by blue sticky notes stuck to some of the boxes.

Upon closer examination, you discover the unmistakable scribbles of hurried teachers ...

In the fiction section some scribbles say:
Bullying Behavior
Swear words - Goddamit and Hell, pgs. 34 & 71
In the nonfiction section, notes say:
Discusses Menstruation

Some Outdated Views on Women
Some gun violence
Uses 'Ass' to Mean Donkey, p. 12

The teacher notes are meant as a friendly *heads-up* so their colleagues can dodge surprises—or teach around—or rethink their pick—or totally ignore the note altogether, all options as they wish. The books aren't covering these topics, some of which could otherwise be good and appropriate picks for 3rd and 4th graders. Still, what this kind of caution means to your ed market publisher and to YOU is that your book may not be used—and there goes your unwavering admiration.

Ed market publishers often play it safe because their books are filtered and purchased by others—typically well-intentioned outsiders—for use by students. The opposite is generally true in trade book publishing, where parents, extended family, or the children themselves filter and select books. This distinction is important in understanding why trade publishers may have more flexibility with sensitive topics. They don't operate under the same process nor scrutiny as educational publishers.

THE EXCEPTION TO SAYING YES

Even though you've been encouraged to say YES to your first, and all subsequent assignments, if you're uncomfortable about the topic just say NO.

Other taboos collected from the School-Of-Hard-Knocks by our educational editor and writer friends are:
Librarian & teacher stereotypes
Sibling name calling
Kids getting badly hurt or physically harmed
Scary text & graphics
Halloween, spirits, underworld
Sarcasm, excessive humor, run-away potty humor

While it's impossible to foresee all matters that *could* be perceived as "sensitive", use your good judgement to steer clear of things that *could potentially* cause problems. This is especially true if the content is not integral to your book. Ask yourself:
Is there anything in my book that could earn a blue sticky note from teachers in the bookroom? Heightened grumbles from parents at board meetings? Thumbs down from administrators at budget time?
Could it trigger unintentional behavior like name calling? Cause any unintended foul-play, like tripping classmates thinking it's funny?

Does it broach subjects that could hijack a teacher's lesson and get her in a heap of trouble?

If you answer yes to any of these questions or others like them, consider making a few mild adjustments so your book sends out positive, thoughtful, and uplifting messages instead. That feels better, doesn't it!

In sum, be sure *all* content in your book is not only free from opinion and judgement but that it considers and respects the age of your readers.

A final point, if you're writing test passages, the guidelines provided to you sometimes specify things to avoid, like experiences that may not be familiar to most children. So your Pâté taste-testing scene in that quaint outdoor café in Paris might have to be swapped out for Peewee soccer practice on a soggy field riddled with mud puddles!

One final sensitivity guideline applies to *all educational writing:* when appropriate, ensure that your work reflects the diversity of our world, thoughtfully and respectfully.

X. TRITE AND OVERUSED

Last, but not least, we should *cut to the chase* about our final writing topic, employing trite expressions and cliches. *In this day and age* we know we should avoid them, so we can *breathe a sigh of relief* that we've finished our topic *where a good time was had by all.*

Augghhh!

Was that last paragraph grating to your nerves? It's chock full of overused trite expressions. These common phrases can stealthily slip into our writing as we type out our manuscript, concentrating on meeting deadlines.

Avoid them. Using common cliches reduces the quality of your manuscript and they *won't pass muster* when crossing your editor's desk. Though we did enjoy writing about this topic knowing that our editor will have to let these clichés through!

XI. ART SPECS – PHOTOGRAPHS – VISUALS

"Art Specs & Photographs & Visuals, Oh My!"

Did we just say that? And immediately following the section on trite and overused phrases, too! Isn't it fun to be a writer?

But let's not digress. Next up is information on the visual aspects of your upcoming educational book. Publisher expectations on these extras vary. Fortunately, everything you need to supply for your manuscript will be spelled out in your guidelines. Well...*mostly.*

First, the publisher may ask you to provide art specifications (art specs) or illustrator notes (illo notes). This means you describe the illustration you want to go along with your brilliant text. A few words or a sentence will do. These are often placed in brackets to separate them from the body of the manuscript.

The same is true if you intend to use photographs. If there are specific requirements for photos you'd like the publisher to use, you'll need to describe them. However, if the photos you have in mind are straightforward or obvious based on your text, notes aren't needed. Your editor will tell you if he needs anything different.

For example, in your book on Invasive Species, the single page on Burmese Pythons in Florida probably won't need a note. On the other hand, if your book is Fun Facts About Burmese Pythons, you'll need lots of photos of the slithering giants— swimming, eating, mating, hiding, etc. For that, you'll add notes describing the pictures you want. Or, you could pull pictures off the internet to give your publisher an idea of what you need. They won't use *those* photos, but they'll have a good idea of what you're looking for.

Generally, publishers will supply *all* the photographs. They have a robust art department and that's their job. But, there are certain projects where this would be difficult, if not impossible.

For example, if you're writing a craft, how-to, or cookbook, you'll likely have to supply your own photos. The art department won't be making Auntie Jane's Dazzling Donuts or knitting a fuchsia sweater just to take a picture. Or, if you're bringing highly specialized expertise to your book in other ways, like

WHEN IN DOUBT ASK

Your Editor can describe or provide samples of anything you need. Remember, don't overdo it, and give them exactly what they want.

noting the Do's and Don'ts of Siberian Horticulture, you'll need to supply photographs for that too.

When Mike wrote a memoir for Heinemann, both he and the publisher wanted it to be as accurate as possible. So Mike provided photographs for the memoir, even though the book was illustrated. In this case, the illustrator used the photographs to ensure the artwork captured the time, place, and events of Mike's story accurately. The result was amazing.

Sandra was asked to supply photographs of professionals she interviewed for her dance book. So, her finished book was a mix of photographs she supplied and others the publisher provided.

Other visuals you might need to consider include graphs, charts, maps, and other elements. You can either clearly describe these in notes, or include a "dummy" which your publisher's art department will use as a guide.

As you can see, your guidelines may not be able to *exactly* spell out everything you need,—especially if your manuscript has unique visual requirements. In contracts, publishers take care of this by referring to the *entire Work* which includes *all materials.* Your publisher is not trying to be sneaky. They simply want to make sure they're covered for anything that goes into the book.

If you've landed an assignment and you're not sure what the visual requirements are, discuss this with your editor up front! You don't want to approach your deadline only to learn it's up to you to provide pictures of Bigfoot in her natural habitat.

XII. GLOSSARY

A glossary is where you define words that might not be familiar to young readers. It will be up to you to choose these words from your manuscript. You'll often be told how many to include, a number which varies among publishers and the projects you work on.

The trick to glossaries is to define the words based on the grade level and subject matter of your book. This means you *do not* take definitions verbatim from a dictionary. Instead, you write them in relation to your manuscript. For example, let's define our sun. If we're writing a book about types of stars, we might say, SUN—the yellow dwarf star in our solar system that is 4.5 billion years old. If we were writing about physical forces we might say, SUN—the star that creates the gravity holding our solar system together.

Generally, *you'll* be asked to provide the definition. Sometimes, your guidelines will state that the editor will provide the definitions.

XIII. INDEX

Indexes are fun! An index is simply a list of interesting words that send the reader to different parts of the book. You have full latitude to choose words that highlight fascinating aspects of your manuscript. You'll want to spread these around, like the questions you will make up next, to cover different topics in your manuscript.

XIV. CURIOUS QUESTIONS

What's in a question? In educational writing, a question fills several needs. It engages readers in an interactive manner, tests how much they comprehend, and detects whether or not they read the entire book.

How do they accomplish such wide and varied tasks?

Because you write them that way! If your Author's Guidelines say to include five questions in the backmatter of the manuscript, then make sure they're interesting and also that they reference topics throughout the book.

Here's a question we might put in our backmatter if this were an educational manuscript.

   1. Who owns the copyright when you sell a manuscript to an educational publisher?

      Answer. The publisher! You learned this information in Chapter 1.

Why did we ask that question? Because it's exactly the type of question you could be asked to write as part of your manuscript package.

When developing questions for your manuscript, the answer should be easily found somewhere in your book. You'll also want to reference where to find the answer. These questions will be used by teachers and educators for homework or classwork. It's important that readers can easily go back and find any answer they forgot.

Your publisher will have guidelines for writing the questions, but it's up to you to make sure they're appropriate for your audience. Let's say you wrote a book on geology.

A question for third graders might be—*What are the three main types of rocks?* The answer—*igneous, sedimentary, and metamorphic (page 7)*. Notice we included a reference page for the reader to easily find the answer.

If the publisher allows a more playful style, we might ask this type of question in a whale book. *Do blue whales have teeth for munching their lunch?* The answer would be, *No. They have baleen, which is a brush-like screen that captures tiny tidbits of prey (page 3)*.

For 5th graders you might ask a more difficult question, like—*How are igneous rocks formed? (page 12)*. This is a more open ended question that requires a short written answer instead of a simple list.

You'll want to spread your questions out. Use questions that review the entire content of your book, not just a chapter or two.

The task of writing questions is quick and fun. It gives you a chance to review your own manuscript and chose specific points you'd like to highlight.

XV. EXTENSION ACTIVITIES

Now that your book has ignited your reader's interest, why not satisfy their insatiable thirst for more?

Great idea!

That's the purpose of Extension Activities. They're easy-to-implement, fun tasks that enhance your readers' new interests, skills, and discoveries. They take readers beyond what they've read in your book in any number of ways. An extension activity might:

- Apply a skill to a real-life event
- Adapt what they've learned to a new situation
- Enrich knowledge by digging deeper into a topic

The possibilities are endless. Extension activities must connect to the content of your book in a manner that will make sense to the reader. They must also be do-able with relative ease and preferably at minimal cost. Even better if it can be accomplished by the reader independently, without adult assistance.

Your guidelines might specify the length and scope of your Extension Activities. This is especially true if you have a book in a series. But other times, these fall into the *entire Work* category and are vague. It's best to get some direction from your publisher before you start. Otherwise, you could waste a lot of time dreaming up a super activity, scouring the Internet for accompanying visuals, and adding notes to describe your exact vision—only to discover that you need a fun, Fun, FUN Extension Activity, not the lab based study you devised.

Oops is probably not the word you'd utter while trashing your 3-hours-in-the making Extension Activity.

XVI. AUTHOR BIO AND PICTURE

Finally! Not only do you have a book with your name on it, the publisher may even ask you for a photo for your author bio. Cool!

Make sure to take a great photo. This is how everyone in the world will see you!

Then on to your author bio. This is your chance to talk about you. Not that you'll be able to highlight your entire career and aspirations. In fact, most publishers provide a tight limit on the length. Two to three sentences seems to be about the norm. But that's plenty to get the point across.

Take some time to thoughtfully consider the content. The bio you write here will be listed in this book…forever!

You should also take a moment to enjoy the thrill of accomplishing this task. The fact is—you've done it! You're an author with a book in print!

Let's change that to: you're an author with your *first* book in print.

More on the way!

XVII. CHATGPT & ARTIFICIAL INTELLIGENCE (AI)

Welcome to the new world! A world filled with computers, databases, and massive computing power. Add these together with the texts of millions of books, articles, essays, and other writing and what do you get—Chat Generative Pre-Trained Transformer, better known as ChatGPT.

ChatGPT is an Artificial Intelligence (AI) tool capable of remarkable things. For example, when applied to the field of educational writing, it can crank out articles, stories, and other written texts on *any* topic, for *any* grade level—*instantly*—literally in seconds! So in the *brief* time you spend complaining to your partner or pet about your uninspiring assignment on gluten or on the complexities of writing your early reader on quantum physics, ChatGPT has already written *both* of them, with time to kill.

"YIKES" you rightfully say.

Indeed, it's true that you, an educational writer, are going to be impacted by ChatGPT and other AI technologies in some way. But exactly how? That's the mystery!

To some Ed market writers, talk of AI triggers sorrowful laments over lost jobs and the inevitable end of work-for-hire altogether. They believe there is no appreciable difference between human and AI-generated writing. Clearly, their water glass is half empty. Others believe the quality of human writing—with its creativity, voice, and spirit—will always prevail over AI-created writing. They are unphased by AI. Their glass is half full, and they're probably wearing rose-colored glasses, too! These are some of the opinions and prophecies of educational market writers. There are lots more.

ARTIFICIAL INTELLIGENCE UPDATE

Warning! This is a rapidly evolving technology that changes quickly. Expect ongoing updates.

And it's not only a conundrum for writers! AI art generators have created an upheaval in the illustration market too! While no one can predict the future, AI will continue to grow and change with time, no matter how empty or full our glasses are. So let's toast to fate and consider how best to move forward. Cheers!

Here are some thoughts:

- Stay informed.
    - ChatGPT and other popular AI tools are like any other resource or technology that might impact your profession, positively and/or negatively. Do some research and discover what's out there.
- Try it out.
    - A basic trial of ChatGPT (you'll find with a simple online search) is presently free, though that may change. As you give it a whirl, consider your own assessment and opinions of the writing. Think about ways you might be able to use it. Can it help you generate ideas or point you in a direction for your research? Maybe!
- Follow Publisher guidelines
    - As ChatGPT has taken the world by storm (yes, we felt this trite and overused cliché was appropriate), publishers have taken notice. References to the use of AI are beginning to show up in their submission guidelines. Some allow you to use it. Others may not. Either way, if you do use AI in your writing submission, you'll need to mention it upfront.
- Use Your Professional Network
    - Staying on top of fast-changing new tools and AI technologies is tricky. That's why it's imperative to be a member of a quality organization like the SCBWI. They offer affordable webinars, yearly conferences, and numerous other ways to keep up to date on industry issues. It's what they do!
- Ethics
    - AI ethics is another matter to consider. Your editor will not be happy if you try to pass off AI-generated text as your own! That's not what they hired you for (with their legally binding contract). AI can be a useful resource, but your original work should be

reliably better and show a level of writing skill and maturity beyond what is presently generated by ChatGPT. That is what your editor is counting on!

Move forward...CAREFULLY! If you do submit to a publisher that allows some use of AI, be aware that AI writing tools can be as wonky as an unreliable narrator! Texts may include errors, omissions, outdated facts and details, and misleading fabrications, which are called *hallucinations*—what a great name! While unintentional, these hiccups highlight the downside of AI-generated text.

While some of you are cheering over these weaknesses, those of you who might use it will want to exercise caution and treat all AI content with a healthy dose of skepticism. Verifying everything with reliable research is a must!

XVIII. ACADEMIC STANDARDS— A BRIEF HISTORY

Here it is! The final section in this chapter... and *surely* the one you've been waiting for! While Sandra totally believes the best topic was saved for last, she also knows that *a lot* of educational writers are not as smitten as she is with the academic standards. Many, like Mike, were practically clueless about them—at first.

So how is it possible to be a successful Educational Market writer without a thorough grounding in academic standards? Because you'll receive everything you need from your editor. This includes guidelines that lay out any academic standards you need to address in your assignments. How easy is that!

Still, there's no harm in having a tiny bit of knowledge in advance. Who knows, you could delight your editor by responding "Yes! I'm *familiar* with the Standards," should she ask. That, alone, makes this section worth reading!

The Academic Standards you'll come across *most often* are the Common Core Standards in Reading. Reading falls into the school curricula known as English Language Arts or ELA. So what are the ELA Reading Standards? They are learning goals that students are expected to meet by the end of each grade, K–12. The intention of the Standards is to set consistent expectations across the states, so all students have the skills and knowledge to succeed in college, in a career, and in life after graduation. It's an easy-to-grasp and honorable intention.

The Standards establish a progression of skill development. As students move from one grade to the next, their skill should grow. For example, in kindergarten, students are expected to identify the front and back cover of a book. In first grade, they expand this skill and are taught to recognize and use a Table of Contents and text headings. By the end of second grade, using captions, subheadings, glossaries, electronic menus, and more is added to their repertoire. At the end of third grade, they are expected to be savvy about sidebars, hyperlinks, and more. This type of progression appears in all of what are referred to as the "Anchor Standards for Reading" which cover all aspects of reading, from *learning to read* to *reading to learn.* The Standards create a framework or structure that aligns instruction across all grade levels. Makes sense, right!

It's important to note that the Standards do not recommend methods of instruction, nor do they specify materials that should be used to teach specific skills and knowledge.

The Standards are not a curriculum, they are learning goals. School districts, school boards, teachers, and parents often have a say in the methods and materials used to teach the standards in classrooms. But back to our lesson.

Forty-eight states adopted the Common Core Standards and fully implemented them on or around the 2014/15 school year. The few states that did not adopt them, created their own or already had their own in place.

For many years, the Standards were followed diligently by most school districts across the nation. But in time, they fell into disfavor. Some believed too much time was spent teaching to the standardized tests—tests that assessed student, teacher, and district-wide performance on the Standards. Others felt the standards were too rigid and did not account for differences among student learners. There were numerous other issues also involved. As a result, many states jumped ship and created their own standards, often modifying the Common Core in ways that parents, teachers, administrators, and State Education officials deemed best.

As an example, New York State now follows the New York State Next Generation Standards. Other states followed suit. Texas, one of the states that did not adopt the Common Core Standards, continues to follow their TEKS or Texas Essential Knowledge and Skills standards.

While we've focused this section on Reading Standards, you should also know that there are numerous other standards. Ones that cover Math, Science, Social Studies, Art, Library Studies, Physical Education, Music, Social and Emotional Learning, and more! All can easily be accessed on the Internet, through state education websites, and/or through your editor (should you need them).

Should you need them? Today interest in STEM instruction which blends Science, Technology, Engineering, and Math is high. As a result, you may receive an assignment where your guidelines include a standard or two from the Next Generation Science Standards. Likewise, Social and Emotional Learning (SEL) is also a high-interest area. Standards or topics relating to this may also appear in project guidelines.

In closing, we recognize that for many of you, dazzling your family and friends—and perhaps your editor with your exciting new insights on the Academic Standards may be the greatest benefit you'll derive from this section. And for those of you wishing to write lesson plans and teacher guides, your experience with the standards, along with your knowledge of grade-level curriculum and content, could help you land a ginormous assignment right away!

No matter which category you fall into, should you be asked if you're familiar with the Standards, you can now shout a big, loud "YES!"

"FIX-UP" WRITERS

Even if this isn't an *official* title, these writers are standouts! They are *reassigned* projects that were not completed or pulled from the original writer, which sometimes happens. If you're a super speedy writer and are willing to take on projects under very tight dead-lines, let your editor know. This skill can help you build long relationships!

CHAPTER 10

DEADLINES AND SUBMISSIONS

I. DEADLINES

One of the sections of your writer's guidelines will list specific dates that are vitally important to your editor—the deadlines for your manuscript. It might look something like this:

Writer agrees to deliver a complete outline of the Work not later than 4/1/2024. The final work, complete in form and content, will be delivered on 4/20/2024. Penalty for delivery more than five days after deadline is 20% reduction in pay. If delivery is more than 10 days late, Publisher has the right to declare the contract null and void.

No question about being wishy-washy here! The deadlines are set in stone and very important to the publisher. They have specific publication dates for your series and for their entire set of releases for that season. If any of their authors run late, it creates problems.

Consider this. You're writing three books of a six-book series. What if the other author runs late on her deadlines? It affects YOUR series release. The publisher only has three books about *Gardening in Space* instead of the six that marketing promised to its buyers. The publisher has already advertised and sold this series to schools and libraries across the country. Oops.

Publishers do not like "oops." That's why the contracts are very specific and include penalties for tardiness. They want you to know they're very serious about having your manuscripts in hand at the proper time.

But what happens if some crazy life event occurs and you know you'll never meet your deadline? Confess! Confess instantly, immediately, and right away. The sooner you let your editor know you have a problem the easier it will be to deal with. Sometimes the editor will be able to give you relief on the deadline dates. If not, it gives her time to assign the project to another author. Dealing with problems up front and openly can keep you on their authors list.

The best thing to do is never miss a deadline. However, if you have to miss one, the way you deal with the problem can easily determine whether or not the publisher will ever assign you another project.

The other side of this issue is when you're the author they contact to write a project with a missed deadline. In this case, you'll have an *extremely* tight deadline for your work. Take a deep breath and check your calendar before you accept a proposal like this. If you say yes, the publisher is counting on you!

Mike had a brush with this type of deadline issue when Rourke Educational contacted him asking him to write three books in a series. The first author had run into a problem and couldn't meet the deadline, only two and a half weeks away. When they offered Mike the project, Rourke suggested a deadline of about five weeks to finish the three books. A great opportunity but also a lot of fast work! It required researching three different facets of outer space; historical perceptions of space, how space technology and exploration affect us on Earth, and the technical aspects of space exploration. All three had tight deadlines for the outlines and completed manuscripts. As you can imagine, he had to find significant time around his work schedule to get everything done. He found a solution by working early mornings and late nights.

His reward for his hard work? The three books were published less than four months after he completed them! Well worth the effort.

Last-minute projects like these can be an exciting part of the Educational Market, but are not for the faint of heart!

II. MANUSCRIPT OUTLINE

By now you've already learned a bit about manuscript outlines. You know what they are, why they are needed, and what could happen if you foolishly think you can skip writing them. Surely you'll recall Mike's Double-Strike-Out in trying to write two books without them. Bad idea—twice!

Here you'll learn even more about outlines. That's because they are your first deadline! Or shall we say your first test at meeting deadlines!

As you'll (hopefully) recall, your outline includes a summary of the manuscript chapters and the topics you intend to highlight in your project. You'll know how to do this because the writer's guidelines explain what is required. If you're not sure, email or call your editor. She'll be happy to discuss exactly what she needs.

Once you've submitted this outline, it'll be a few days before the editor returns it. She'll want to make sure it's what the publisher needs, and also that it's aligned with the other outlines—outlines from authors writing the remaining books in the series.

Inevitably, you'll be asked to make changes to your carefully prepared outline. There are lots of reasons for this, none of them relating to your skill as a writer. They may want more "people profiles" or coverage of other topics or a different angle on certain subjects. It's part of the process to make several changes to what you had initially planned.

Where you'll sometimes run into a problem is when the publisher starts a completely new series. On the plus side, you're the author of books in a brand new series...Hurrah! On the negative side, the publisher has given you guidelines for your manuscript, but decides to change them after you've already written it...Dang it!

The best advice we can give is to think Zen and deep breathing. This too shall pass. It's inevitable. Any series that has been published for years has a clearly defined format and tone. Editors are pretty clear on what they're looking for. With a new series, editors will try to improve it during its birthing process. They might be dealing with school standards that are changing, new requests from their senior editor, or simply might not like the original concept they had devised. It's your job as an author to do your best to fill their needs.

Remember, they also have deadlines to meet, so there's a limit to the changes they'll ask for.

III. MANUSCRIPT FORMATTED AND COMPLETE

"I think I can!"

"I think I can!"

If you're chugging along, thinking *maybe I can get this done after all*—you're on the right track. Just push on ahead!

Once you've started, you'll find that steadily chugging forward, bit by bit, will get the job done. It will move you along the process for getting to a completed manuscript, which is pretty well defined. It starts with your outline. That outline goes to your editor, who will send it back to you asking for changes. You'll complete her requested changes and return it. If you have any questions at all, send an email immediately! She'll get right back to you.

Once your editor is happy with your outline, you'll dive into the project. Depending on your personality, you might want to write the manuscript using a basic Word document format first. This allows you to write in a way you're familiar with before getting deeper into the required formatting.

Sandra opts for this method. In addition to postponing formatting matters, it allows her to save copies on her computer in a convenient format. She finds it helpful as she wrestles the content of her manuscript into perfection. She then transfers her work to the publisher's required format after she's done.

Mike uses a slightly different method. He writes his first draft as a typical Word document. After that's edited, he makes a properly formatted copy and does all future changes in the publisher's requested format. When he's ready to send it on to his editor, the document is ready to go.

As you become more comfortable with your educational writing, you might simply write the manuscript within their specified formatting guidelines from the very start.

Next comes the collaboration with your editor. You'll send her the completed manuscript and she'll ask for changes. This will probably go back and forth two or three times if your communication is reasonable and you're fulfilling her requests.

Ultimately, you both agree on the final product and your project is on its way to production.

That's it! Your manuscript is complete!

YAY! Again you dance around the living room. Ruffle the dog's fur. Pet the cat. Hug your spouse. Cheer with the kids. And this time have some cake and ice cream because you've lost 10 pounds getting this far! You did it! Mission complete!

Oops!

Except... it's not!

III. PROOF COPIES

One very important check remains. You need to make sure the proofs are accurate.

Proof copies are the finished product with all art and text put together in the proper book format. It IS your book in an electronic format, probably sent to you as a PDF. Sometimes they will be marked up by your editor with notes on a few final changes.

It's normally a month or two after you finish your manuscript that this will show up in your email. As usual, your editor will give you a *very* tight deadline to look at it! Probably just a few days, certainly less than a week. It will likely arrive just as you start your Hawaii vacation, celebrating the fact that you're now a published author. But even if you've planned your days full of sightseeing, snorkeling, and sampling the local food, you must examine it very, very carefully!

This is your FINAL chance to catch any errors and ensure your book is something you will be proud of. Think of it this way. If your name is misspelled or one picture's caption has been switched with another, that faux pas will last FOREVER in your newly minted book!

CHAPTER 11

WHAT'S NEXT?

I. INVOICE—SHOW ME THE MONEY!

Now that you've written a book, you'd like to get paid! This won't happen automatically in Educational Publishing. You are an independent contractor working for the publishing house. They appreciate the work you've done, but the finance people won't send any money your way until you send them an invoice and ask for it.

What does an invoice look like?

The publisher may have one in your author's guidelines. If not, then simply search online for a basic invoice template, and change it to fit your needs. All you'll need to list is the publisher, your address, the book you wrote, and the amount the publisher agreed to pay. List this important number under *amount due!*

Now patiently wait a few weeks and a check will magically appear in your mailbox. Or, as publishers begin to embrace technology, you may have the option of a direct deposit. That works, too. Either way, you get paid!

Hurrah!

II. AUTHOR'S COPIES

It might be a few months or it might be a year later, but the big day *will* arrive—the day you receive your author copies in the mail!

This day is the result of long hours of hard work—frenzied worry, late nights, early mornings, stressful emails, tight deadlines, and ultimately satisfying accomplishments. The final step in your long path to becoming a published author. It's the fulfillment of a dream.

Surprisingly, this will happen without any fanfare or warning at all. You won't receive a note from the publisher or an email from your editor. A package from the publisher will simply arrive in the mail one day.

But that doesn't take away any of its importance. You'll know what it is when it arrives and it's fun to treat it accordingly. Don't open it right away. Get one of your kids or a friend or life partner to take a video as you open the package. Enjoy their oohing and aahing as you take out the book. Hold it up and memorialize your expression on this important day. You've reached an incredible goal that likely took you years to achieve.

You deserve to enjoy the moment.

YOUR BOOK

The arrival of your author's copies will probably be the first notification that your book is now in print. Congratulations!

III. TAXES

As an independent contractor, you will receive a tax form 1099 from the publisher sometime in early February of the next year. This notes the amount of money they paid you and *must* be included in your taxes!

Don't neglect to do this. Uncle Sam will notice!

IV. JOB CYCLES

Now that you're a published author, the Educational Publisher you wrote for will be clamoring for more of your work. Excellent! Right?

Well. Maybe.

Educational Publishers tend to work in cycles. They may search for authors once a year or twice a year, probably not more than that.

If your editor liked you and you did a great job, she may have an offer of work for you every cycle. Maybe one book, maybe three.

However, keep in mind that there are lots of other authors clamoring for work. If your editor has projects better suited to others, she may not have work for you in the next cycle.

Then if you haven't worked for a cycle, you might fall to the bottom of a long list, lost in the mix.

Mike has had experience with this both good and bad.

With Rourke, he continued to get projects on a semi-regular basis. His editor liked him, he did a good job, and he always met deadlines. But it only lasted a few years. Why?

His editor moved to another publishing house. When that happened, his consistent work dried up. He was later called by another Rourke editor to do some last minute work, which he successfully accomplished. But after he declined a project a few months later he hasn't been contacted again. It's a fickle business!

Stories like this are commonplace. When an editor moves, her favorite authors may not be on the front list at the publisher any longer. Only if she moves to a similar position in a similar type company might she have the opportunity to offer more projects. This is an unlikely scenario.

Another situation occurred when Mike wrote for Fountas and Pinnell, another great educational publisher. They had put out a call for writers for poetry, nonfiction, and fiction, to be written at 3rd and 4th grade reading levels.

Mike sent in his samples, including some poetry and nonfiction. The editors liked his work so much that over the next four months he wrote four poetry books, a nonfiction book, a fiction book, and a memoir in verse. Incredible!

Obviously they've called him for several projects since then. Right?

Wrong.

Since Fountas and Pinnell update their reading program books on a specific schedule, it may be several years before they do their next update in the 3rd–4th grade level. Mike hasn't heard a word from them since his project was complete.

Talk about a roller coaster ride!

You will also come across "jobbers' in the educational publishing industry, also referred to as "packagers" or "content development houses." Some educational publishers, instead of finding their own writers, will contract that work out to a jobber. A jobber finds authors to write books for different publishers. That means jobbers provide lots of jobs! Red Line is one jobber that provides this service for children's book educational publishers. Each publisher still has editors overseeing the process to ensure the final product meets their standards, but your primary editor and contact will be provided by the company who hired you. What does this mean to you as an author?

It means more work opportunities but lower pay.

Now back to our story. Mike wrote several books for Red Line as he was breaking into educational publishing. Since then, he's focused more on Trade publishing and higher paying educational publishing jobs, but he has never burned any bridges. Once or twice a year he is offered projects by Red Line, which he has turned down for the past few years. However, if the right project is offered, on a topic he's fascinated by, he'll be happy write another book for them. Each time he is offered a project, he politely declines, but requests to stay on their list.

This interaction recently worked out well for both Redline *and* Mike. When Redline offered Mike the opportunity to write more books, he accepted two of them. This allowed Mike to be completely current in the educational market as we prepared this book for print.

For you, as a new author, it's best to take any assignment that comes your way. Once you're established in the industry, you'll determine exactly what type of projects are the best fit for you in the future.

V. ACADEMIA AND LESSONS

Some academic educational publishers who create lesson plans, teacher guides, and other curriculum projects also operate in cycles like their traditional counterparts. But a few academic content development houses work on a different system altogether. These houses competitively bid to create *large* curriculum programs for other companies. These could be small private companies or large, well-known literacy giants. The companies may not have an internal staff big enough to tackle a large job, or they may already have a project in progress and must outsource job #2 to meet deadlines. Content houses are awarded a contract based on cost, speed, quality of work, and other criteria. Once awarded a contract, they will often schedule writers for 3 or 4 fast-paced, totally engrossing months at a time to get the job done.

"SHUT UP!" You say. "A THREE or FOUR month project?"

How will you attend your planned Lost Weekend Get-Away with college roomies? The week-long reunion event celebrating your 80-year-old great grandmother's fifth wedding? Or your daughter's out-of-state oratorical competition, which is *not* to be missed?

No need to worry! The editors ask about conflicts before bringing you onto the project and they work hard to schedule around you. They'll consider solutions like a later start date, splitting the work between two writers, etc.

For example, due to a schedule conflict, Sandra was brought onto a team a week after a project launched. The project was a unique online phonics-based reading program for grades K–2. It was under a very tight deadline. She was responsible for creating all the student lessons for grade 1, a total of 27 lessons. Each lesson included simplified instruction, interactive practice and review activities, fun sidebar tips, and an interactive test. The lesson content was fed into an online template. In addition to creating the lesson, Sandra also selected all of the artwork from a large database provided by the publisher for each lesson. Completing two lessons a week, which included some back-and-forth exchanges for slight edits, while working full time kept Sandra busy!

These massive school-based educational projects are completely different from the straightforward book writing projects we've focused on. With these larger projects, Sandra intentionally accepts no more than two per year and is highly selective. High interest, intrigue, and enthusiasm are a must. Once you work your way into the system, you can do the same!

Another difference with these large-project jobbers is they have a *very* direct approach to finding and assigning writers—it's all about speed.

Here's how several publishers do it. You submit your name and contact information along with the topics and grade levels you're experienced in. You'll also answer questions about what template formats you know, what submission and tracking programs you've used, and what group communication tools you're familiar with. For each answer, you'll indicate your level of experience from low to high. They also ask how willing and eager you are to learn new programs. Everything is added to their database and updated on an annual basis through email.

Enter—a new project. All the editors (who are working on *many* projects) will have access to your entire file, in fact, to the entire database of writers! They search for the skills they need for their new project, and—voila—your name pops up. A quick email later and you're accepting your first project. Or your third. Or tenth!

Sandra has been contacted by editors both old and new when her publisher is hiring writers for a new project. She has also been contacted by editors who have moved to other companies. Think about that! It's a real bonus to be offered work from a company you've never pitched to! As Mike says, don't burn any bridges. Keeping those bridges intact will facilitate navigating your future path to on-going work assignments.

BEHEMOTH BURNOUT!

Taking on too much, too often, can lead to burnout. While you may have the occasional crunch time, you should wisely guard against burnout. You can't afford to let the quality of your work falter.

VI. STAYING CONNECTED

One great way to stay at the forefront of getting jobs, is to stay in contact. If you've already written a book, you know an editor! Stay in contact by sending her a note once or twice a year expressing your interest in writing. Or if you've developed a more familiar relationship, you might even trade occasional emails on other topics.

If you haven't published a book yet, then stay "in contact" with publishers by following them on Facebook, Instagram or X (formerly Twitter). Social media is where a publisher will make announcements about authors and books. More importantly for you, it's also where they might send out a call for authors when they have work available. You want to be first in line!

There's no need to follow *all* the educational publishers.

That would be nuts, not to mention time consuming. Plus it would take away from your writing time. Follow only those that really interest you. You can always swap them out for others or add more in the future. Fickle? Perhaps, but your time is too valuable not to play the field a bit.

Keep in mind, if you send a submission packet out and get a response like *"Nothing at this time"* or *"Nothing now, but I'll keep your name on file,"* you'll want to stay in contact. Not like a stalker, but a note every 3–4 months should keep you on the list.

Another angle you can take is to do some serious online searching for industry insiders.

To discover these resources, you'll have to dig to find the gold (or diamonds, depending on your personal preference). Some of their noteworthy news might cross your social media feeds, but mostly you'll have to take the initiative and seek out these rich nuggets yourself. Use all of your newly honed research skills to make sure you're following true industry experts and not slick wannabes.

Here are a couple examples of industry experts "in the know."
- Harold Underdown
  - A longtime guru of children's publishing. He's the author of *The Complete Idiot's Guide to Publishing Children's Books,* Executive Editor of an Imprint of Astra Books for Young Readers, and he has a website chock full of good stuff! Harold is *committed* to keeping children's writers informed of new start-up imprints that are *eager* to find new authors like YOU! He also shares updates on the whereabouts of industry professionals. Great! It's a way to track

editors if they change companies, which happens a lot! Follow Harold on any of his social media platforms or on his website.

- Jan Fields & Paula Morrow
    - Dynamos in the field of educational publishing. They've hosted the 5-day *Educational Writing Workshop* at the Highlights Foundation every summer for years! It's the premier workshop on writing for the Educational Market—hands down! Over the years, Jan and Paula's Workshop has helped many writers enter the marketplace and grow successful writing careers. This is how Mike got his start! If you want to extend your knowledge beyond this book, get current on trends in the market, and take advantage of door-opening opportunities from industry insiders, you should consider attending their workshop. Learn more about Jan and Paula and the Highlights Educational Market Workshop.
- Shameless Plug Here for Mike and Sandra
    - Mike and Sandra have recently expanded this successful Highlights' tradition by teaching an incredible, amazing, fantastic, *online version* of the Highlights Educational Workshop. Well, at least *we* think it's pretty good. With this annual 8-part webinar (complete with industry expert guests), insider information on the Educational Market is now accessible by anyone around the world. We look forward to seeing you there! That's it. Shameless plug complete.

When you're finished searching for industry insiders, it's time to schmooze! Not with the industry insiders. Not yet anyway. But with any connections you've already made.

Network. Network. Network! Being in the right place at the right time matters. Once you've connected with others in the business, networking extends your reach—it's like hanging around a watercooler of educational marketplace gossip and other good stuff, including news about new available projects.

A quick way to launch your networking initiative is to join a selection of listservs and social media platforms for children's writers. The friendly kid lit community keeps up on industry news and will make you aware of calls for open submissions and more. There are a lot to choose from. They range in size from small regional groups to large national outlets. Sandra follows Work-for-Hire Children's Book Authors & Illustrators group, Writing for the Educational Market Slack group, KIDLIT411, NFFEST, SCBWI regional groups, and some regional school and academic groups. Mike is electronically stunted and follows only what Sandra or his wife tell him too. Then he rarely checks the feed. This has probably led to several missed opportunities!

If you're interested in test preparation and other kinds of academic writing opportunities, you'll want to join LinkedIn, a business and employment-focused media platform. Be sure to list your interests in receiving news on jobs relating to educational writing. That way Linkedin will let YOU know when companies are looking for writers. Many writing jobs that were once on-site in larger companies are now offered as "work-from-home" or freelance opportunities. More and more, companies are following this trend. There is also a sudden BOOM in companies creating new educational programs. Many are trying to fill academic gaps. Others support home-school students and programs. LinkedIn is where demand for educational writers flourishes.

The perfect opportunity may await you there!

Joining professional organizations is another way to connect. Some offer job posting information and networking that could lead to job opportunities. But be careful of scams! Do your research!

Two well respected organizations are:
  • Society of Children's Book Writers and Illustrators (SCBWI)
    • This is the leading professional association for serious children's writers. Becoming a member, is a MUST! They hold events, conferences, and webinars, and have regional chapters which are ideal for networking. In terms of locating work, the SCBWI publishes four e-newsletters on industry events, *The SCBWI Bulletin, Insight, La cometa,* and *Pro-Insider.* The SCWI Blueboard is an industry discussion board they maintain.

- Editorial Freelancers Association (EFA)
    - This professional organization serves a broad and very specialized audience of freelance writers. Their jobs posting service is available to members and covers open searches for everything from medical writers to copyeditors for college level physics textbooks to Siberian horticulture how-to's.

This start-up list of ideas to stay connected is just the beginning. Naturally you'll want to keep enriching it with new prospects, both from your diligent research and from all of your wonderful soon-to-be successes.

VII. EDITORS THAT MOVE

Most editors are wonderful people who are thrilled to be working with authors and developing great books for kids. It's a great collaboration for a wonderful cause.

Unfortunately, editors have a major flaw—they are real people! They have goals and dreams. They have to balance their work lives the same as we do. They want to advance to better positions or find a better work/life balance.

So what's the problem?

The problem for authors is that in order for your editor to get a higher paying or more fulfilling job, she may have to move to another publisher! This happens quite frequently. Your wonderful editor who loved your work so much might take a different editorial job that deals with college level physics or tropical fungus research.

Congratulations to the editors who are able to do that! But DRATS for us authors who have lost a connection to the market.

Notice we said "lost *a* connection to the market"—not *all* connections! After you've pounded your fists, screamed at the sky, and ranted to your significant other (who nods politely), update your submission materials, and begin over. It's called picking up the pieces. Embrace it.

VIII. SPREADING YOUR WINGS
TO THE TRADE MARKET

The longer you write for the Educational Market, the more you'll start glancing at the Trade Market. As you do this, you'll figure out a few important facts.

First, the Trade Market pays much better. Instead of buying the copyright for your manuscript for a one time payment, Trade Market publishers copyright the manuscript in *your* name. They make money by signing a contract with you that allows them to sell the book for you. In return, they pay you a royalty for each sale, typically about 10-15% of the retail price (to be split with the illustrator).

You'll also notice there is a lot of overlap in the markets. Many nonfiction Trade books look suspiciously like Educational Market manuscripts. And educational fiction has plenty in common with trade fiction.

Finally, you'll see all of them turning up on Amazon and other booksellers. In the past you rarely saw educational series outside of a school. Now you'll find your Educational Market book appearing on Amazon in electronic format. Unfortunately you don't reap any financial reward from this, simply the satisfaction of seeing your book on display.

So why doesn't everyone write for the Trade Market? Because it's incredibly difficult to sell your manuscript there!

It's simpler to break into the Educational Market because their books will turnover in school systems quickly enough to create lots of new projects. They also have strict author guidelines and carefully structured texts, which make it easier for editors to work with less experienced authors.

To break into the Trade Market, you'll need to write an entire manuscript hoping that it's what an editor is looking for.

If it isn't, you won't get any feedback at all. Simply a lack of a reply. This makes it very difficult to determine exactly what the publisher didn't like. Without that type of feedback, trying to improve your next manuscript is difficult.

The good news is that the practice you get writing for the Educational Market will teach you skills that make all of your manuscripts more appealing.

Using these new skills, as well as critique groups, mentor texts, and connections with other writers, you'll have a much better chance of selling your other manuscripts in new markets.

IX. PITCHING A SERIES

SERIES WRITING SAMPLE

Sample appears in the Appendix.

Now that you're familiar with the Educational Market, we have some *great news*—there's another way to pitch your work! We didn't mention this earlier for fear you would collapse with excitement and render yourself unable to read the book.

The fact is, some educational publishers are interested in hearing pitches for new *series.* That's right. They want you to plan out an entire new series for them to publish! Wow!

Can you imagine a better way to start your writing career? We can't! Woo-Hoo!

But wait a minute.

If this sounds too good to be true, it's because it *mostly* is. Although this is a bona fide method of pitching to the Educational Market, it's not likely to be the easiest way to sell your first book. Many of these series are developed by authors who already have knowledge and experience with this type of work.

But hey. You're motivated. You're skilled. And you have a great idea that the publisher will never be able to pass. If that's the case, then read on.

Pitching a series to an educational publisher requires a different type of submission process than what we've discussed. Let's translate that into writers' language—you'll have to do more work!

First, you'll need to come up with a brilliant idea. This brilliant idea needs to work for a typical series of at least four books. Something like, *The Points of the Compass, North, South, East, and West.* This could easily be made into a series of four books, one for each direction of the compass, although it sounds terribly boring. Let's try another one. How about, *Furry Nightmare Creatures.* Write a book each on *Bigfoot, the Chupacabra, a Werewolf, and Giant Rats.* If the series does well, the publisher can always add the *Abominable Snowman* and other fearsome furry critters to the series.

Once you have your idea in hand, it's time for... more research! You want to make sure any publisher you pitch doesn't already have a similar series in print. Also, plan on using a comparable word count to a series the publisher already has.

With that complete, it's time to start writing. You'll need, at a minimum, a riveting query, an overview or summary of the series, a complete outline of the first book, a list of the planned books in the series, and the level you'll be writing them at. You may also need a couple sample chapters from the first manuscript, if not the entire thing. Check submission guidelines for exact requirements. If you're pitching to a publisher that does *not* list submission guidelines for a series (which is most publishers), here's what you'll want to include:

1. A riveting, intriguing, amazing query
2. An overview of the series and characters
3. The level you'll be writing at (include the name of the publisher's imprint for the appropriate reading level)
4. A list of the first four books in the series
5. Your manuscript
    a. For shorter works (about 1500 or fewer words per book) include the complete first manuscript.
    b. For longer works, include at least the first two chapters.

That's it! Nothing to it, right?

If you're wondering about *our* experience with this, we haven't had much luck. We've pitched Rourke Educational and ABDO with different projects, to no avail. Our only reply... crickets.

However, it wasn't all bad news. We pitched one of the series (and sold it!) to Astra, a Trade Market publisher. We had to rework our original idea and reformat it significantly to make it a perfect fit for Astra—but the added work, and rework, and "creative flexibility" (a term we've come to appreciate) resulted in a *fantabulous* new opportunity—a series sold to the Trade Market. Persistence pays off!

CHAPTER 12

Onward!

Congratulations! You made it!!

You've put in massive amounts of time and effort. You've researched companies and books and reading levels. You've written fiction or nonfiction, poetry or lesson plans, reader's theater or maybe a series about different types of smelly fungus.

WHEW!

You deserve a well earned pat on the back and a cold brew of your choice—kombucha, soda, wine, tea, or an ice cold beer. Sit back, relax, and wait for the good news to roll in.

And while you're waiting...

We're especially thrilled to note that *our* ending is *your* beginning!

You've taken a major step on your way to becoming a published children's book author, or perhaps a respected team member authoring concise lesson plans for our next generation.

You've also entered a bold new market that's as vibrant and dynamic as your own hopes and inspirations! We may not be able to tell you what the future holds, but today the Traditional Educational Publishers are already:

- Exploring new avenues of entering the Trade Market.
- Publishing new genres like novels in verse and graphic novels.

- Covering emerging, current and timely new topics.
- Learning to engage young readers in ways that excite them today!

The Academic Market segment has:
- New models of instruction that drive innovation in exciting directions. Interactive instruction is bursting with new programs that engage kids in new learning experiences.
- Self-paced, individualized, responsive instruction to fill gaps in student learning and address today's generation of students—these digital-savvy, visual, and voracious consumers of all things fast-paced.

The future has yet to be written and YOU are a part of it. As you set off on your journey, stay alert, look for new opportunity, and enjoy the adventure along the way!

Welcome to the Wonderful World of Educational Publishing

Mike Downs   *Sandra K. Athans*

Mike Downs   Sandra K. Athans
mikedownsbooks.com   sandraathans.com
mikedownsbooks@gmail.com   sandraathans@gmail.com

IT'S A WRAP!

We're excited for you and wish you much success!

ED MARKET BOOK ATTACHMENTS

Here are the attachments you've been waiting for! *Actual, true, authentic, bona fide original* queries, resumes, writing samples, interview requests, and more!

Queries

Writing Samples

Resumes

Interview Requests

FAQ's (Dueling FAQ's by Sandra and Mike)

QUERIES

General Query for Educational Work—Mike Downs
   • *In this query, Mike emphasizes his aviation (technical) background, his education, and his ability to meet deadlines.*
   • *This query (accompanied by two samples) resulted in a two-book deal.*

Rourke Educational Media

Dear Submissions Editor,

I'm contacting you to express interest in writing for Rourke in the Grade K-6 level. I am interested in your non-fiction as well as leveled fiction readers. I included one sample of each, as well as one aviation themed sample.

I'm particularly interested in writing on any aviation related topic. I'm a lifelong aviator who has flown aircraft from F-15 fighters to airliners to hang gliders. I believe I could bring a clear voice to this market.

My qualifications include: USAF Academy graduate, aviation science masters' degree, fighter pilot, and American Airlines' instructor pilot. I've written two aviation themed non-fiction books for the trade market and I'm familiar with writing manuscripts on different reading levels. I also have expertise and interest in writing about many other topics (see attached resume and included writing samples).

My experience as a military officer makes me comfortable following guidelines and meeting deadlines.

Thank you for your time and consideration.

Mike Downs

General Query for Educational Work—Sandra K. Athans

• In this query, Sandra emphasizes her knowledge of Rourke, her teacher's credentials, her writing background, and the fact she'll have enough time to write even though she works full time.

• This query, along with samples, resulted in two projects acquired.

Rourke Educational Media

Dear Editor's Name,

I am a fan of Rourke's Classroom Collections, having used many of your company's books in my lessons and in my after school clubs. The "Seeing Both Sides" series stirs my students as we tackle opinion/argument writing; and "The Time Hop Sweet Shop" series is a new treat for my Historical Fiction Club, Grades 2 - 3. I would greatly enjoy contributing to the wonderful resources Rourke makes available to educators and kids!

While I am a practicing writing teacher (Grades 2 - 6) and a teacher trainer, I still have over twenty hours a week available for writing projects. I understand that you are currently looking for nonfiction writers, and I would welcome the opportunity to assist Rourke Educational Media in this capacity. I have pub-lished nonfiction books, articles, and plays and have attached (below) a select list of these together with examples of my nonfiction writing for children. I have also attached a fiction sample should you have a need for this in the future. I have an advanced degree in Literacy from Le Moyne College and a BA degree in English from the University of Michigan, Ann Arbor. My resume follows.

As I tell my students, the secret to success is to blend fun with learning! Rourke books do just that! They're a great read and an informative read, as well. A quick book chat on any of the Rourke works I use during instruction is an 'easy sell' to any of my students! Thank you for that! I also greatly appreciate the currency of your works. The Next Generation Reading Program is tuned-in and timely.

Thank you for your kind consideration. I do hope there might be some future Rourke projects that you feel will align with my knowledge and talents. I look forward to hearing from you.

All best,

Sandra K. Athans

General Query for Educational Work—C. Rowen MacCarald

- *In this query, Rowan emphasizes a conference connection, teacher's credentials, previous educational books, and the ability to write at different levels.*
- *This query, along with samples, resulted in several projects.*

Good Morning,

I enjoyed hearing Roger Rosen talk about Rosen Publishing at the 21st Century Children's Nonfiction Conference last month. I would love to work with your company on a project.
As you can see from my resume below, I'm a freelance writer with an M.S. in biology. I've written four educational books for third to sixth graders on a work-for-hire basis, all of which are currently in print. Two had topics related to social studies and two involved both history and engineering.

I included two unpublished writing samples, one aimed at middle graders and the other at young adult readers, at the end of this email. You can also find links to some of my nature and science articles for local papers on my website (website.com).

Thank you for your time. I look forward to hearing from you.
Sincerely,

C. Rowen MacCarald

Specialty Query for NOVEL IN VERSE—Brian Montanaro
- *In this query, Brian is pitching a specific novel in verse.*
- *This query (along with its writing sample) resulted in a sale.*

Ten-year-old Arlo didn't want to follow in his big sister's shadow on the basketball court. He wanted to do something different. Something he could call his own. But playing ping-pong in the basement is not the same as the Olympic sport of table tennis. Arlo plays table tennis once a week in a small gym with a group of players older than his dad. While they help improve Arlo's game, it's not until after his father takes him to the larger club near his sister's college, that Arlo realizes he's not the only kid who takes ping-pong seriously. Between Arlo's long-distance relationships with his new best friends and the lessons from the coaches he gets when visiting his sister, he not only becomes the best player where he lives, he slowly works his way up the national tournament ratings. But the more he travels and the wider group of people he meets, the more he realizes that ratings aren't everything. In the end, the people he meets along the way and the encouragement he gets from his parents, and even bonding with his older sister, mean more to him than the game.

MY OWN SPIN is an 8,000-word MG novel told in verse. Having reached a high level in the sport of basketball, I'm enjoying learning something new. But table tennis is unlike any other sport I've experienced. Even though it is not as popular in our country as many others, at a recent table tennis camp, I met people from over ten different countries and so many different walks of life. It is the only place where age or where you come from doesn't make much of a difference. I've lost matches to both ten and eighty-year-olds. But no matter your skill level or where you're from, someone is always happy to lend a helping hand. My 500-word sample is attached. Thank you for your time and consideration.

Sincerely,
Brian Montanaro

Specialty Query for SERIES—Jan Fields
- *In this query, Jan is pitching a specific series.*
- *This query resulted in a sale of the series.*

SERIES PROPOSAL: SAVED BY PIRATES

SERIES OVERVIEW
Reading Level/Grade 2. Characters age 11–14. 4 Chapters.
Word Count 900–1000.

The series focuses on *The Angry Ghost,* a pirate ship crewed
by an unusual group of young people. The crew of *The Angry
Ghost* doesn't see themselves as pirates forever, they just want
to gather enough treasure to afford a home of their own where
they, and kids like them, can finally be safe, but they'll do
almost anything to achieve that goal.

MAIN CHARACTERS:
Elizabeth/Jinx: an orphan who runs away to avoid a beating
and ends up aboard a ship of teenaged pirates.

Captain Benjamin Small: the pirate captain who fled abuse of
his own. He is quick and smart and utterly fearless.

Bug: Though born without legs, Bug more than pulls his weight
aboard the ship as an inventor. It is his inventions that have
allowed the *Angry Ghost* to sail with such a tiny crew. Give Bug
tools and time, and he can build you the world.

Jerry: No one climbs or fights better than Jerry, the daughter
of the dread pirate, Mighty Jack. She joined Captain Small's
crew because no other ship wanted the wiry girl with a bad
attitude. She is Benjamin's good right hand in any fight.

Apple: He does all the cooking aboard the Angry Ghost, and
no ship at sea eats better. Apple is the biggest guy on the ship,
and he can fight if he must, but he's happiest when he's cooking.

BOOK SYNOPSES

BOOK ONE: *The Jinx*
When Elizabeth flees from a beating, she sees stowing away on a merchant ship as her only hope of escape. Unfortunately the ship encounters a horrible storm and Elizabeth is discovered hiding below deck. The crew is sure the jinx of having a female on board is causing the storm and put her off the ship in a tiny boat that promptly capsizes in the storm. She nearly dies until she is rescued by the crew of the Angry Ghost.

BOOK TWO: *Haunted*
While sailing back to the pirate cove they consider their second home, the crew of the *Angry Ghost* finds the other pirates in the cove in a panic. It seems a ghost ship has been visiting the cove in the dead of night. And when it leaves, pirates are always missing. Can the crew of *Angry Ghost* put a stop to this ghostly raiding?

BOOK THREE: *Never Give Up*
When a new gang of vicious pirates boards the *Angry Ghost* and takes over. They put the crew in a small boat and leave them, triggering some bad memories for Jinx. But she's not alone this time and the crew of the *Angry Ghost* isn't about to let anyone take what's theirs. What they lack in size, they more than make up for in smart and sneaky.

BOOK FOUR: *Payback*
While the *Angry Ghost* is moored in the hidden pirate cove to restock water and food, they learn that the ship that tossed Jinx overboard is not far away. Wouldn't it be great if their next horde of booty came from the very people who nearly killed Jinx? The crew thinks so, but how does a crew of kids defeat seasoned sailors? Very carefully.

OUTLINE BOOK ONE: *The Jinx*

Chapter One/Run-Away: After cook prepares to give Elizabeth yet another beating, she escapes and runs. For a while, cook gives chase, but she isn't nearly the runner than Elizabeth is and soon Elizabeth is alone at the docks, determined that she'll never go back to that kitchen. She'll never be beaten again. Then she spots a ship, bobbing quietly in the calm waters. And Elizabeth sees her chance.

Chapter Two/Out of the Frying Pan. When the hold where she is hiding springs a leak during a terrible storm, Elizabeth is found and dragged out of the hold and onto the deck of the storm-tossed ship. The crew of the ship is certain that having a female on board has jinxed them and demands she be cast overboard.

Chapter Three/Into the Storm: The captain clearly doesn't want a young woman's death on his head, but he knows his crew will mutiny if he doesn't do something so he sets Elizabeth adrift in a small boat with only a single flask of water and a package of hard biscuits. Her boat bobs helplessly in the rough water and soon capsizes. She loses her food and water but manages to cling to the overturned boat. But how long can that last?

Chapter Four/The Pirates: Just as Elizabeth is certain she can hold on no longer, she is rescued and hauled aboard the pirate ship, Angry Ghost. But as soon as the crew hears that she was cast overboard as a jinx, they laugh. The Angry Ghost is full of misfit pirates are misfits, all with a plan to gather enough booty to open a real home for kids like them. A place they can be safe, so this jinx should fit right in.

BOOK ONE: The Jinx
Sample Chapters

Chapter One: Run-Away

Smack! Smack! Smack! The heavy stirring stick hit Cook's hand over and over. "Come out, girl! Come get what's coming to you. It'll get worse if you make me wait."

Elizabeth huddled in the dark space between the cast-iron stove and the wall. She would not come out. She would not be beaten. Not again.

"It wasn't my fault," Elizabeth whispered. Her voice so low it was barely a breath in the darkness.

She had not meant to drop the teapot. A mouse had run up her skirts. Elizabeth remembered the maids giggling as she slapped at her dress.

No one laughed when they saw the dent in the silver teapot. They knew what it meant. They'd all felt the heavy hand of Cook before.

But Elizabeth was *never* going to feel it again.

She bolted from her hiding place and raced by Cook. She was fast. She almost made it. A heavy hand grabbed the back of her ragged dress.

Elizabeth twisted and kicked. The big woman howled. Elizabeth raced out the door and through the garden. She ran in a blind panic down street after street.

Cook chased her, but she was too old and too slow for the chase.

Elizabeth ran until the stench of dead fish made her gag. She was at the docks. She knew stories about the docks and dangers that lurked there. Elizabeth didn't care.

She looked at the wooden ship bobbing quietly in the water. All Elizabeth saw was escape.

Chapter Two: Out of the Frying Pan

Elizabeth clung to a heavy crate as the floor under her feet tilted hard.

The ship around her groaned as if the storm hurt. Icy salt water poured in from cracks in the side of the ship. The water soaked her shoes and the hem of her dress.

Not for the first time, Elizabeth wondered if she would die here. She had hidden for weeks of terror and sickness. Now all the hiding seemed pointless. Surely the ship would be torn apart by the storm.

The floor tilted again, slamming Elizabeth against the crate. She whimpered at the fresh pain.

Then Elizabeth heard loud voices. Frozen in fear, she peered into the shadows. She had to hide.

Small crates slid on the floor with each tilt of the floor. Any one of them was heavy enough to break her ankle if they hit her.

The door to the hold flung open. Two men staggered into the hold. They saw her in seconds.

"A stowaway!" a tall man shouted. "A girl."

The other rushed at Elizabeth. "Jinx!"

The men were wet to the skin. They dragged Elizabeth out onto the deck. "This is why the storm attacks us," the tall man shouted. "A jinx."

"Throw the jinx overboard!"

"It's our only hope!"

Elizabeth looked around at the angry faces. Finally time to die, she thought.

WRITING SAMPLES

Fiction Sample—Mike Downs

Mike Downs
emailaddress@gmail.com
ph 555-555-5555

377 words/Lexile 500L-600L
Unedited FICTION sample

ALLIE IN TROUBLE AGAIN

Mrs. McMurphy wagged her pudgy finger inches from my nose. Her face glowed the same bright red color as the ribbon I'd stuck on Tommy's back.

"Young lady!" she bellowed. "You apologize to Thomas Chadwick III."

I wanted to scream. Tommy had stuck that very same ribbon on me out on the playground. But Mrs. McMurphy would never believe me. Everybody thought Thomas Chadwick III did no wrong.

Tommy shifted back and forth, staring the meanest stare he could muster. I called him Tommy because it made him crazy.

Putting on my 'oops I'm in trouble again' sorrowful look, I turned toward him.

"Tommy, I'm ..."

"Ahem!" Mrs. McMurphy wagged her fingers at me again.

I restarted my apology. "Mr. Thomas Chadwick III," I said, mimicking the voice of a butler, "I sincerely apologize for decorating your boring shirt with a beautiful red bow."

"Mrs. McMurphy!" he yelled. "That's not an apology." He held the red bow, shaking it back and forth. He tried to throw it at me, but the tape kept it stuck to his hand.

"Calm down," said Mrs. McMurphy, "or I'll send both of you to the principal." She pulled the bow off Tommy's hand.

I didn't want to see the principal again, so I moved to step two of my plan.

"I'm sorry Thomas. I shouldn't have put the bow on your back."

Mrs. McMurphy nodded. "Very good. Now both of you back to class. I don't want to see you again."

We turned away. Tommy broke into a big grin as soon as we moved out of earshot.

"Hah! That was a great apology. I love it when you have to say, 'I'm sorry Thomas Chadwick III," he gloated. "I always win in the end."

I shook my head. "You're right. You always win." I secretly slid my hand in my pocket where I had a special surprise. I brushed against Tommy from behind. That was step three of my plan.

"You'll never get the best of me!' he said, chuckling.

I squeezed my lips together holding back my giggles. As he walked into class I looked at the note stuck on the bottom of his pants.

It said, 'Tommy eats beetles. YUM!'

Fiction Sample—Sandra K. Athans

• Note that this sample is not a complete story but a single chapter.

Sandra K. Athans   Unedited Fiction Sample. 4th Grade
emailaddress@gmail.com   Chapter 1. Word Count:
ph 555-555-5555   300/Lexile 500

CAMP HOBBY HORSE
Chapter 1: Barn Buddies

Olive held her breath.

Miss Ivy's pointed finger was so close to her nose, her eyes crossed.

She waited. She wiggled like a worm. Until...

"BALONEY!" Miss Ivy said. "YOU get Baloney!"

"YIPPEE!" shouted Olive. It was a dream come true!

The Icelandic pony's real name *Skeönie,* was hard to say. Everyone called him *Baloney.*

Now Olive would be taking care of him. She was one of three new stable helpers at Camp Hobby Horse. She couldn't believe her good luck!

Olive watched Miss Ivy call out the next pair.

"Izzy. You get Applesauce." Izzy squealed in delight.

Only Ziggy remained. Olive wondered if he would get Freckles or Boomer.

Miss Ivy pointed from Ziggy to a shaggy old mule in the corner. It lazily snapped at a pesky fly sending loose hairs flying off its coat like blown dandelion seeds.

"Grumbly is yours," she said.

Ziggy's eyes went wide. Olive and Izzy gasped. What had poor Ziggy done to deserve Grumbly? She felt bad for him— and also a little relieved for herself!

Miss Ivy ignored the fuss.

"Remember, these buddies aren't final until after Try Outs," she said.

Earlier, Miss Ivy told the helpers about the Try Outs. They would have to feed, water, and brush their buddies under her watchful eye. She also told them about Swap Outs. If the buddy fit was good, there would be no swap outs. But if it wasn't....

"Let the Try Outs begin!" said Miss Ivy wasting no time.

The three flew into action, starting toward the hay bales.

As they did, Olive had a horrible thought. If she didn't do everything right—*perfectly right*—she could end up with Grumbly!

Jan Fields   Word Count 268/Atos 2.5/Lexile 348
emailaddress@gmail.com   Beginner Fiction Sample
ph 555-555-5555

RUN AWAY PIZZA

Piggle has a growly tummy. "I will make a pizza."

Piggle opens cupboards. Piggle checks in drawers. He finds cheese, but no toppings.

"I will make cheese pizza."

Piggle rolls the pizza round and flat. He spins the pizza faster and faster. He throws it high into

the air. The pizza flies up, up, up. It flies right out the window. It flies into the sky. Where will it go?

"Stop that pizza!"

Piggle runs through the garden. He squishes the vegetables. He slips and slides.

The pizza flies on.

Piggles climbs a tree. Up, up, up he climbs.

The pizza spins and spins.

Piggle grabs the pizza. The pizza is floppy. It is not white. It is not plain.

"I have pine needles in my pizza," Piggle says. "I have bugs in my pizza too. Yum!"

He carries the pizza into the house. He presses it into a pan. He adds flat vegetables from the garden. He adds cheese. He pops the pizza into the oven. "I will invite my friends to have pizza."

Piggle puts on his hat and coat. He goes outside to find his friends. His friends are there. "We saw you running," said Dash.

"We saw you climbing," said Bear.

"We saw you grab a floppy bird," said Duck.

Piggle laughed. "I did not grab a floppy bird. I grabbed a run-away pizza."

Dash shakes his head. "Silly Piggle. Pizza doesn't run or climb or fly."

"Mine does," says Piggle. "But it is not flying now. It is ready to come out of the oven. Time for a pizza party."

Yay!

Nonfiction Sample—Mike Downs

• Note the sub-headings used to break up the sample into easy-to-read chunks.

Mike Downs
emailaddress@gmail.com
ph 555-555-5555

510 words/Lexile 500L-600L
Unedited NONFICTION sample

THOSE PESKY MOSQUITOS

Bzz. Bzzz. Bzzzz. Whap! Missed again.

Those pesky mosquitos never stop. They're always buzzing around looking for a place to land. Why? Because you're a walking restaurant. They make a quick landing, a jab through the skin, and ahhh. Mealtime. A tasty treat for the mosquito. An itchy spot for you.

Mosquitos and Water

All mosquitos live near water. That includes more than 3,000 species found around the world. If you're near water, a mosquito is near you. Mosquitos lay their eggs in water. They prefer to lay eggs on water that's not moving. Ponds and puddles are great. Old tires or cans are fine, too. There are probably mosquito eggs near you right now. Most females lay 100 or more eggs at a time. These are laid together as a raft or a floating ball on the water. The eggs take about two days to hatch.

Snorkeling and Wiggling

Mosquito larvae (**lahr**-vee) hatch from the eggs. Many hang under a snorkel tube called a siphon. They use the siphon to breathe. That means most mosquitos snorkel before they fly. Larvae move by jerking their bodies back and forth. This jerky motion gives them their nickname, wigglers.

All wigglers shed their skin. This is called molting. They molt exactly four times. After the fourth molt, the mosquito larvae become mosquito pupae (**pyoo**-pee). Mosquito pupae dangle in the water, too. But they breathe from holes in the back of their neck. No snorkeling for them.

Flying and Food

The adult mosquito grows inside the pupal skin. After two to four days, the skin splits. Then the adult mosquito pulls itself out and flies away. That's when it looks for you.

If a mosquito bites you, it's a female. Most females need blood to lay eggs. She bites using her proboscis (pro-**bah**-sis). She presses the proboscis to your skin. Under this proboscis is the fascicle (**fah**-sih-kul). The fascicle goes into your body. Does it hurt? Nope. It's so tiny you don't feel it at first.

A mosquito might gulp blood for a minute or longer. Some eat more than their own body weight in blood. Imagine trying to eat your own body weight in food. What a stomach ache!

Mosquito Danger

Are mosquitos dangerous? Yes. Mosquitos have caused more deaths than lions, sharks, earthquakes, volcanoes, and car accidents combined. They're dangerous because they transmit diseases like malaria, yellow fever and dengue. Malaria alone kills more than a million people each year. That's more than all the people in the state of Alaska.

Avoiding Mosquitos

How do you stop these diseases from spreading? Get rid of the mosquitos. This is done by draining water from places where mosquitos lay eggs. Or by putting a special oil on the water so mosquito larvae can't breathe. Some people raise fish that eat mosquito larvae. Pesticides are also used.

But what if a mosquito is chasing after you? Hopefully you're using insect repellent and wearing clothes that cover your skin. If that doesn't work, there's only one thing left to do...

Bzz. Bzzz. Bzzzz. WHAP! Try not to miss.

Nonfiction Sample—Sandra K. Athans
• *Note the exciting sub-headings.*

Sandra K. Athans
emailaddress@gmail.com
ph 555-555-5555

450 words/Lexile 600L-800L
Unedited Nonfiction sample

AT THE BOTTOM OF MT. EVEREST;
The Other Great Adventures of Edmund Hillary

Edmund Hillary is best-known as one of the first climbers to reach the *top* of Mt. Everest. But he felt his greatest achievement took place at the *bottom* of the mountain—building schools and hospitals for the families who live there.

EXTREME CLIMB

WHOOSH! Howling winds slammed into the canvas tent. SWOOSH! Dangerous gusts whipped the flimsy shelter. The tent sat perched on an icy ledge near the top of Mt. Everest—the highest mountain on Earth.

Inside, Edmund Hillary and Tenzing Norgay got little rest. At three o'clock in the morning, the freezing sub-zero temperatures became unbearable for sleeping. It was time to gear up.

The men squirmed out of sleeping bags and then dressed in thick layers of clothes. They donned bug-eyed goggles and Darth-Vader-like oxygen masks.

Looking like space aliens, they began their final struggle to the top of Mt. Everest. No one had ever made it to the summit. Dozens had tried. Fifteen had died in the attempt.

TOP OF THE WORLD

The pair strained in deep snow. They hacked out a path. They clawed their way up booby-traps of ice-slick obstacles. One wrong step and they could tumble to their deaths. One misplaced swing of an ice axe and an avalanche could sweep them away.

The summit grew slowly closer. Would they make it to the top or would they die trying?

At 11:30 am, on May 29th 1953, they stood together on top of the world. It was the achievement of a lifetime.

But Edmund Hillary would later say his proudest accomplishment happened *at the bottom* of Mt. Everest. There, he did something extraordinary.

SOMETHING IS MISSING

[SIDEBAR: THE SHERPAS]

The Sherpas are an ethnic group that live in Nepal. Many work as mountain guides. Tenzing Norgay was a Sherpa.

Hillary treasured his strong friendship with the Sherpas. He wanted to help them in any way he could.

The Sherpas desperately wanted a school. There were none. Their children had no way to learn about the world or to study for good paying jobs. Hillary knew what he had to do!

He sprang into action! He raised money to buy building materials. He searched out a Sherpa teacher. Then in 1961, with the help of the Sherpa families, he built the first school.

It would eventually change thousands of lives for the better. Girls and boys could learn many things. A nickname for the school quickly took hold...

THE SCHOOL HOUSE IN THE CLOUDS

The School House in the Clouds.

Three girls and thirty-seven boys attended when it opened. But that was just the beginning.

[SIDEBAR: SCHOOL UPDATE]

Today over 60 schools educate thousands of Sherpa children.

BIG HEART

Edmund Hillary died in 2008. He is remembered by most people for his summit of Mt. Everest—Yet to the Sherpa families living there, he is remembered for his kind heart.

Edmund Hillary once said his work for the Sherpas had given him "more satisfaction than a footprint on the mountain."

• This sample is 660 words, a higher word count than we suggest, but it worked just fine!

ONCE UPON A SLOTH
by Rowen MacCarald

Sloths. Slow. Hairy. Adorable. Giant.

Wait, giant?

Once upon a time, giant ground sloths roamed the Americas. It all started long ago.

Thirty-five million years in the past, the globe looked nothing like it looks today. South America floated along Earth's crust with no connection to North America. On that lonely continent of South America, ground sloths evolved.

As millions of years went by, ground sloths slowly changed. Ground sloths lumbered in the lowlands and scaled high cliffs. In huge and empty deserts along the coast, one kind of sloth stumbled on a new way to eat: underwater.

As big as shaggy cows, marine sloths drifted along the seafloor munching sea grasses. Their bones evolved to become denser to help them sink. For millions of years, ocean-going sloths plied their trade.

Other ground sloths crossed an ocean rather than swim beneath it. Starting at the coast of South America, sloths paddled north from island to island. Eventually they reached North America. The wandering ground sloths encountered new creatures in their new home, such as horses and saber-toothed cats.

Eventually, Earth changed. Land rose out of the sea between South and North America. By three million years ago, the two continents had joined together. The new land altered the flow of the Pacific Ocean, making the waters colder and emptier. The sloths who once feasted under the sea died out.

Other sloths survived. They waddled north along the land bridge to join the sloths that had already settled a new world. Other animals, such as wolves and bears, moved in the opposite direction to colonize South America.

More and more sloth species evolved across the Americas. Some stood on two legs to reach into tall trees for leaves and twigs. The two largest species towered over 10 feet (three meters) in height. The biggest ground sloths could look over a woolly mammoth's head.

In some parts of South America, ground sloths were skilled diggers. They plowed through rock and dirt. Some sloth-made tunnels were five feet (1.5 meters) wide and many hundreds of feet long.

Predators hesitated to attack the lumbering giants. A sloth's long claws, meant for grabbing food or digging burrows, could be as deadly as giant knives. Some species had claws over a foot (0.3 meters) long. Some ground sloths wore armor under their long fur. Small bits of bone studded the sloths' skin, making it hard for predators to take a bite.

Fifteen thousand years ago, Earth changed again. The most recent Ice Age was coming to an end. The glacier covering most of North America was shrinking. Newly ice-free land gave humans a way to reach the continent on foot or by boating along the coast. People soon met their first giant ground sloths, and sometimes ate them.

Temperatures rose. Forests grew thick, and other habitats changed. Within a couple of thousand years, humans with their hunting spears spread all over the Americas.

Soon after humans showed up, ground sloths disappeared. So did other huge animals, such as mammoths and Ice Age bison. Scientists aren't entirely sure why. They don't know whether the end of the Ice Age, the arrival of humans, or both pushed the giants to extinction. But by around 10,000 years ago, every ground sloth species on the two American continents had gone extinct.

Some kinds of ground sloths clung on for a bit longer. Humans hadn't reached some islands in the Caribbean, which may have protected the animals. The largest Caribbean sloth was about the size of a small black bear.

Humans eventually arrived on the islands of the remaining ground sloths. By 4,000 years ago, the last of the ground sloths had died out.

All modern sloths today live in trees in Central and South America. They are slow, shaggy, adorable, and small. The largest sloths are the size of medium dogs. Yet even the pygmy sloth, which is about the size of a house cat, is related to ancient giants.

Specialty Nonfiction Sample POETRY— Mike Downs
  • *This sample resulted in three poetry books.*

Mike Downs
emailaddress@gmail.com
ph 555-555-5555

510 words/Lexile 500L-600L
Unedited POETRY sample

WHAT FLIES LIKE THAT?

Swirling rotors spinning 'round,
Slowly rising off the ground.
Up and down in little hops,
Landing on the building tops.
What flies like that?

A HELICOPTER
Helicopters are special. They can take off straight up into the air. They can land straight down. A helicopter can even land on top of a building. No runway required. Most airliners need a mile of runway to takeoff.

Bubbles full of heated air,
Rise aloft as people stare.
Drifting slowly, floating by,
Ornaments against the sky.
What flies like that?

A BALLOON
Balloons are wonderful, colorful flying machines. In 1783, the Montgolfier brothers sent the world's first passengers up in a balloon. The passengers were a duck, a rooster and a sheep. The 8-minute flight was a complete success.

Off a cliff it starts a flight,
Soaring like a giant kite.
Pilot hanging just below,
Putting on a thrilling show.
What flies like that?

A HANG GLIDER

Hang gliders look like kites but fly like planes. Otto Lilienthal is famous for designing and flying some of the earliest hang gliders, over 120 years ago. He even built his own hill, so he always had a place to launch. Many people still learn to fly hang gliders by running down hills.

*　　*　　*　　*　　*　　*

Speaking of the wild blue yonder,
Here's a riddle you should ponder.
If building planes was up to you,
What would YOUR invention do?

Specialty Fiction Sample READER'S THEATER—Sandra K. Athans

• *This sample has not landed any projects...yet!*

<table>
<tr><td>Sandra K. Athans
emailaddress@gmail.com
ph 555-555-5555</td><td>450 words/Lexile 500L-600L
Unedited Reader's Theater
Skit sample</td></tr>
</table>

Title: The Ugly Duckling Alien
Grade: 4
Genre: Reader's Theater
Word Count: 450
Message: Using your imagination can turn a sticky situation into an out-of-this-world performance.

THE UGLY DUCKLING ALIEN

Characters:
Jerome
Will
Setting:
School

Jerome: It's horrible! My life is over. I don't want to be the Ugly Duckling. Why do these things always happen to me?

Will: It's your own fault, Jerome. That's what you get for trying to hide under your desk.

Jerome: *Now* you tell me! Everyone else was raising their hands. I ducked down to hide and Mr. G. spotted me. How could he ignore all the kids who *wanted* to play the lead role?

Will: Probably your butt sticking up in the air was too hard to resist.

Jerome: Thanks, a lot. *That* makes me feel better. Now I'll be The Ugly Duckling the rest of my life.

Will: Probably. Unless...unless we make it super cool.

Jerome: Super cool? You're kidding, right? Since when is an ugly duckling cool?

Will: Since I came up with my new master plan. An Ugly Duckling rewrite of universal proportions.

Jerome: That would have to be a rewrite of *MEGA*-universal proportions. I hope it works. My life depends on it!

Will: Here it is Jerome. It's done! The new script is perfect, The Ugly Duckling Alien. You're the astronaut hero who lands on the planet Stinkersville. It's populated with unfriendly warty purple aliens. You are the ugliest creature they've ever seen.

Jerome: How can *I* be ugly if *they* are the warty purple aliens?

Will: Because to warty purple aliens, only warty purple aliens are beautiful. A human astronaut is ugly. Very ugly. Not only that, but *you* are the alien on their planet.

Jerome: Wow! What a mind-bending twist. Then the aliens put me in a zoo where they all gawk at me, the ugly astronaut. Right? How do I devise an escape plan?

Will: Easy. These aliens hate poetry, so you'll torment them with verse. Since I've heard your poetry, I know for a fact that anybody on *any* planet would be happy to get away from it.

Jerome: I'll pretend I didn't hear that. Anyway, every time an alien stares at me in the zoo I'll say:
>Warty aliens with onion breath,
>release me from the zoo.
>Otherwise, I'll never stop

repeating this to you.
Stinky sneakers, smelly socks,
moldy beetles in a box...

Will: STOP! Enough already! *I'll* release you from the zoo if the aliens don't. Worst poem ever!

Jerome: Thank you. I know you mean that in the best way. And when my poem drives the aliens crazy, they put me back on my rocket ship.

Will: Right. And instead of being an Ugly Duckling Alien, you're a Handsome Astronaut Adventurer returning to Earth.

Jerome: I like it! Hey, what about Mr. G? Should we tell him we changed the Ugly Duckling script a teenie, tiny bit?

Will: Hmm. He might be a little bit shocked if we don't. What do you think?

Jerome: I think...I think we should make sure someone has a camera focused on Mr. G's face on Parent's Night. We'll get the best picture in the universe when he sees...

Jerome and Will: "Welcome everyone to Parent's Night and our production of:

The Ugly Duckling...ALIEN!
THE END

RESUMES

Resume—Mike Downs

Mike Downs
Street
City, FL 12345
emailaddress@gmail.com
555-555-5555

WRITING LEVEL: K-4

AREAS OF EXPERTISE

Aviation	Fighters, Airliners, Sailplanes, Hang Gliders
Martial Arts	1st Degree Black Belt Tang Soo Do, 2nd Degree Tae Kwon Do, knowledge of Jeet Kun Do, Hapkido, grappling, and stick fighting
Hawaiian History	Raised in Hawaii, studied early texts... Kamakau, Fornander
Finance	Management/Finance Major
Eclectic Skills	I juggle, unicycle, hacky sack, kiteboard, hang glide, surf, boogie board
Riddles/Rhyme	Picture books, several additional unpublished riddle manuscripts.

AREAS OF WRITING INTEREST

Aviation
Fiction Writing_Leveled Readers, hi/lo
Rhymes, Riddles
Life Science, Nature, Oceanography, Space Travel, Physics
Service Academies, Military
American History, Chinese History, Hawaiian History
Martial Arts, Extreme Sports, Circus, Unusual Skills

EDUCATION

1977-1981	USAF Academy, Business/Finance Major
1985-1987	Embry Riddle University, Aviation Science Masters' Degree

WRITING CREDITS

2002-2018   Writer, Picture Books

              PIG GIGGLES AND RABBIT RHYMES,
              Chronicle Books, 2002
              THE NOISY AIRPLANE RIDE, Tricycle Press, 2003
              YOU SEE A CIRCUS, I SEE...,
              Charlesbridge, 2004
              Co-developer of Growums.com parent/child
              gardening program, 2009

AWAITING PUBLICATION

2019   YOUR BODY ON GLUTEN...ABDO
2020   SCIENCE OF THE SUPER BOWL...ABDO
2020   AVIATION, SPACE, COMBUSTION ENGINE...
            Rourke Educational (3 books)
2020   YOU SEE A ZOO, I SEE..., Charlesbridge, 2020

Resume— Sandra K. Athans

Sandra K. Athans
Website.com
555.555.5555
Street.
City, NY 13037

TEACHING EXPERIENCE
Classroom Teacher & Literacy Specialist - PreK through
Grade 5 (15 years)
PreK - Elementary-level academics (Reading, Writing,
Social Studies, Science)
Academic support for struggling, reluctant & second
language learners

CHILDREN'S PUBLISHING (Selection)
Benchmark Education
Simon Says and The Verb Game, Grades 3-4; Word Plays
Reader's Theater
Bully on the Coal Strike of 1902, Grades 6-8, Famous Person
Reader's Theater
Rosen Publishing
The Common Core Readiness Guide to Reading Series
(Grades 4 - 6)
Rosen Interactive eBooks: Common Core Lesson Plans
(60+ Close Read Lessons)
Millbrook Press, A Division of Lerner Publishing Group
*Tales From the Top of the World: Climbing Mount Everest
with Pete Athans*
*Secrets of the Sky Caves: Danger and Discovery on Nepal's
Mustang Cliffs*
AppleSeeds, Highlights for Children - *Mr. Everest, Helping
Hands for the Holidays*

EXPERTISE & WORK EXPERIENCE

- After school clubs: drama, comic book, graphic novels, historical fiction, writing, reading, business, spelling, science, magic, crafts
- School government, campaign activities, public speaking, persuasive speaking
- Competitions: spelling, debates, writing, oratorical
- Children's horseback riding summer camp - coed - family business
- Instructor: Horseback riding, swimming, boating, arts & crafts
- Recreation: Sports, talent shows, themed dances, hiking & camping
- Cabin counselor - care and supervision of 7 - 10 year old girls

EDUCATION & CERTIFICATES

Le Moyne College, Syracuse, NY (MS Education)
Manhattanville College, Purchase, NY (MA Teaching)
University of Michigan, Ann Arbor, MI (BA English)
National Board Certified Teacher:
    Literacy/Reading-Language Arts

Resume (Teacher Centric)— Felicia E. Marquette

Felicia E. Marquette
FMarkell@gmail.com 555-555-5555

EDUCATOR PROFILE

Classroom Teacher, Grades 2 & 3 – Three years instructing
inner-city students in core curriculum
English Language Learning Support, Grades 2 - 4—Afterschool
literacy support & homework help
Academic Intervention Support, Grades K - 4—Writing across
the curriculum
Science Fair Coordinator & Grade Level Representative—Science
Technology Support, Grades 2 - 4—Troubleshooting Computer
Lab instruction
Lesson Plan Design

AREAS OF EXPERTISE

Disabilities Specialist
Support for English Language Learners—Spanish speaking skills
STEAM Enrichment Coordinator—Introduced Global Citizen
Science Projects into School Curriculum
Environmental Center Intern—Summer Internship working with
marine animals
Social & Emotional Learning Yoga Certification, Grades 2 - 4,
Yoga Institute of America

COMMUNITY INVOLVEMENT

Parents as Reading Partners (PARP) Events—Community Library
Literacy Program to assist multicultural families with reading &
writing—Community Welcome
Girl Scouts—Mentored participants with activities

Environmental Activist—Initiate & organize Community Earth Day Activities
YMCA Volunteer, School-Age Program—utoring math, English Language Skills
Children's Librarian Assistant—Reading Time for grades PreK - 3
Waterfront & Equine Counselor—Camp Hobby Horse, local summer camp

INTERESTS & HOBBIES

Poetry Slams, Board Games, Puzzles, Nature Crafts
Hiking, Camping, Outdoor Cooking, Tracking
Rock Collecting, Coin Collecting
Historic Sites, Battle Re-enactments, Museum Collections, Antique-Collecting

EDUCATION

Masters in Literacy Education (Birth – Grade 6) SUNY Oswego
Professional Certification in Childhood Education & Student with Disabilities (Grades 1 – 6)

PUBLICATIONS

Community Reporter—Family articles
School Newsletter—Grade level representative, communicating school events to parents
Online Teacher Blog—various articles on teaching Spanish-speaking students
Teacher-Pay-Teacher—resources for teacher instruction, Grade 3

INTERVIEW REQUESTS

Sandra K. Athans
Interview request letter
   • *Sandra interviewed experts in order to write a book about the amazing Mustang Caves in Nepal. Here's a sample letter.*

Hello Dr. Aldenderfer,

My brother, Pete Athans, suggested I contact you about a children's book on the Mustang caves I'm writing for Lerner Publishing. Briefly, Lerner publishes high-quality, photo-informational books for the library market. Pete and Liesl fully support the project.

The work will feature events from the 2007 - 2012 expeditions (as recounted by Pete, Liesl and their young children) yet also includes informational passages of interest to children in grades 4 - 6. Among other topics, I wish to include short passages on some of the scientific exploration and dating techniques used on the caves and the artifacts and human remains recovered during the expeditions.

I would greatly appreciate speaking with you about these topics as they are among your areas of expertise. I would also welcome any details you would like to share about the challenges you faced during the exploration.

Might I contact you over the phone (or with specific questions through email) within the next several weeks for a 10 to 15 minute conversation?

I thank you kindly for your time and consideration.

All best,
Sandra Athans

Mike Downs
Interview request letter
    • *Mike interviewed four experts in order to write a book about becoming a Respiratory Therapist. Misty, the primary contact, was incredibly helpful and knowledgeable. She notified other therapists who actually contacted Mike via email.*

Dear Misty Carlson,

Good morning Misty. I am Mike Downs, a children's book writer (mikedownsbooks.com). I live in Port Orange, and just signed on to write an educational book about becoming a Respiratory Therapist. The book, BECOME A RESPIRATORY THERAPIST, will be an addition to the *Skilled and Vocational Trades* series of Bright Point Press. The book will be released in Spring 2024, about 7 months.

Here's a link to the current series
    - *the link was included*

I was wondering if you might know of any Respiratory Therapists who would be willing to give a twenty minute telephone interview discussing her/his experience with this career (I came across your name in reference to the Respiratory Care program at Daytona State College). The interviewees will likely be named and quoted in the book. I would like to interview 2-4 professionals in total, and it doesn't matter if they are new to the career or highly experienced.

I would be conducting the interviews before this week.

Please feel free to call, email, or text me if you have any questions or suggestions.

Thank you for your consideration!

Mike

Mike Downs
555-555-5555
mikedownsbooks@gmail.com
mikedownsbooks.com

QUESTIONS I WOULD BE COVERING
1.   Your preferred name and title.
2.   Who do you work with and for?
3.   Does anyone work for you?
4.   Typical schedule? Can you do 3 12's? Shifts?
5.   What training and certification is needed?
6.   Typical patients.
7.   What is a typical day?
8.   What is a special vignette that happened?
9.   Do you freelance?
10.   Travel?
11.   Risks? What did covid do?
12.   How are new people mentored?
13.   Intriguing event or story?
14.   Quotes!
15.   Anything YOU want to say about it?

Sandra K. Athans
Interview follow-up letter
  • *Sandra followed up after interviewing professional dancers to make sure her work would be correct. This is an abbreviated sample.*

Hi Ryan and Alex—

I've prepared several statements from our interviews (below) and hope to use one or two from each of you in the book, depending on space. While there will likely be edits for space as well as to ensure grade level appropriateness (words, sentence structures, etc.), I'll do my best to preserve the integrity of the statements. Also, having several to choose from allows me flexibility when production puzzles together the components of each page.

Please take a look at the statements and let me know if I've captured everything correctly and to your liking. Also, please check the manner in which I've sourced your statements (which follow the statements) to ensure I've listed your name and other details correctly. I am not able to list specifics of your performance credits but can include general accomplishments. You can use another color for edits.

Thanks so much! Truly a pleasure to speak with your both and grateful for your kind assistance in helping others get that much closer to realizing their dreams!

Sandra

Only a single statement is shown from each artist. The actual email included more.

Ryan's statements:

"Finding an agent is one of the hardest things for young or "green" performers. My college arranged a "showcase" in New York City where all acting and musical theater students performed to an audience of over 100 agents. From this, I was able to get a list of the ones who were interested in me. Although I didn't end up getting an agent from showcase, I had a lot of names and addresses. Every six months, I would email and update them on what I'd been doing. I told them I was still seeking representation, and I always asked to set up a meeting."

—Ryan Mac, is a New York City based actor, singer, dancer, and pianist

Alex's statements:

Alex Aquilino covers five different roles in a popular Broadway musical—he's a "swing" and fills in when a cast member is out of a show due to injury, illness, or other emergency.

"Swings have to be dedicated to learn and perfect the roles of the cast [ensemble] they cover—down to the smallest details. It takes talent, drive, and a special skill set to be a swing. It can be stressful but also fun and exciting."

— Alex Aquilino, is a Broadway performer, and he has toured with the national tour of Flashdance the musical

FAQ'S

Dueling FAQ's by Sandra and Mike

Q: How do you balance tight submission deadlines with the need for thorough subject research (nonfiction)?

Sandra:
Plan and conduct focused research from the start. Select 3–7 credible resources (gov., edu., institute, etc.) and try to stick with primary resources. If you get stuck locating facts or verifying discrepancies, you may need to alter or let go of some content. Keep your editor posted, if needed. BTW...all this assumes you've done a *few* hours of preliminary research to find an angle or slant to your book. Once that's done, you must avoid rabbit holes!

Mike:
Do a quick internet search to get an overview of your subject. Then get the information you need from reliable websites only. If you're not sure it's correct, don't use it.

Q: Is it worth hiring a lawyer to review your contract with an educational publisher?

Sandra:
While it's always good for you to read (and understand) your contract, the benefits of hiring a lawyer simply aren't there. The publisher owns all rights and pays a standard flat fee. That's that.

Mike:
No. It's not worth it.

Q: If I landed an assignment to write an article on a topic such as *Animal Shelters,* can I write another article or passage on the same topic for another publisher?

Sandra:
You'd have to be careful that the new work couldn't legally be considered a "Derivative Work". It would have to have a completely different focus.

Mike:
Don't do the same topic unless it's a completely different angle.

Q: I get I'm supposed to say "YES" to any assignment. So it's better to take any assignment, even if you might not do it well?

Sandra:
NOPE! Take any assignment *and* do it well. If you're not familiar with a topic or if the topic is in an area that doesn't align with your strengths, you'll have to take on the burden of additional research. *Your submission must shine!* If you're really, really sure you want to pass on a project, you might pass along the name of a reliable Ed market writer you know. Even then, you may not hear from them again.

Mike:
Sandra is 100% correct (but don't tell her I said that). Your project *must* shine! If you don't think it will turn out well, don't take it! Write a very nice note to the editor saying you're not able to take *this* project but you would love to be kept on the list for future work. I've had good luck with this approach.

Q: I work full time. How do I manage my workload?

Sandra:
Select 5 or 6 publishers you like, submit your Introductory Packets to them, and sit tight for a few months. On average, approaching this many publishers may net you 1 response. After your first few assignments, you're better able to judge what will work for you. Until then, take it slow.

Mike:
Only take one project your first time. Plan on getting up two hours early or staying up two hours late for a few weeks while you're getting it done. After that, you'll know what to expect and how to manage your time for future projects.

Q: Will the publisher ever change what I've written?

Sandra:
Yes, they may. Should this happen, a good editor will typically come back to you and briefly share why they plan to make a change. You may get to make your case for leaving it as written, but in the end, they'll do as they please.

Mike:
Yes! They *can* change your manuscript after it is final. With photo-illustrated-nonfiction the changes likely won't even be noticeable. I did write several poetry books for a publisher and told them they couldn't have the manuscripts unless they made no changes. The editor honored my request, but this is *not* the norm!

Q: Could I publish my Ed Marketing materials under a pen name?

Sandra:
Yes. You could write under a pen name. Some writers use a pen name for their educational writing and their real name for their trade books. Yet, using one name for both is typically more helpful than harmful. You're building credibility as a *published* author of children's books. I use my own name for both.

Mike:
You could, but why? I use my own name. It looks better on the resume.

Q: When working with an editor, how do they typically respond to the items you submit (outline, manuscript, etc.)?

Sandra:
They often use a combination of margin comments and different colored fonts (or highlighters) for in-text changes. They may also summarize ideas in an email or note, too. Review all their changes right away and be sure you understand them. Also be sure to turn around any necessary changes they require in a timely manner.

Mike:
Ask your editor this question! I was so totally clueless for my first few books that I didn't even know my editor had put margin notes in my Word document. Who knew you could put margin notes in Word? I kept submitting revisions without knowing what my editor had said. It's amazing I got *any* more work! Sandra finally realized what I was doing and showed me where to look—after laughing a lot.

Q: Is it helpful to have a social media presence for educational writing?

Sandra:
While most educational writers have some social media presence, it isn't exclusively for their ed market writing. Presently, there's no real benefit. However, writers trying to break into trade publishing often amp up their sites for a variety of reasons: build followers, land an agent, and eventually help support sales and marketing. Also, sales of Ed market books to the public through AMAZON and other outlets *may* change the role social media plays in ed market publishing.

Mike:
No. It doesn't help. Except to highlight your resume as a children's book author.

Q: If you pitch a series that gets accepted & published, will they keep you on as a work-for-hire writer if the series ultimately bombs?

Sandra:
Pitching a series that gets picked up by a publisher is rare! However, if you're among the lucky few who lands one, and it bombs, the publisher's disappointment—lost time and money—will probably linger. Whether or not they keep you on as a writer would be entirely up to them. The take-away from this question is never oversell your series when pitching it. Don't claim it's something it isn't. You rarely get a second chance when you don't deliver on a proposal.

Mike:
I don't know. But I think if you pitched a new series that the editors loved, they would try again. If a series went to market and then bombed, it's the fault of the editors and publisher as much as the writer. My first trade book, Pig Giggles and Rabbit Rhymes, did poorly, but I recently sold another book (which they love) to the same publisher.

Q: Adding the right kind and right amount of humor seems tricky in ed market publishing, especially while sticking to other rules for the market. How can we play it safe?

Sandra:
First, review the tone of other books they've published. Try to get a feel for the type of humor they accept, such as word play, understatement, etc. Use techniques they've ok'd in other books. You can also try other techniques that seem a good fit. Just be prepared for edits.

Mike:
Like Sandra suggests, write your book in the tone already being used in the publisher's series. If it's a new project, use your favorite humorous writing style and let the editor make any changes.

Q: If I'm interested in writing lesson plans or teacher materials, how do I know which state standards my lessons should address?

Sandra:
You will be given all the information you need about standards from your editor. It's not necessary that you seek these out on your own. It's important that you know there are school standards, yet your editor will fill you in on any you might need to write your lesson.

Mike:
I am totally clueless about lesson plans. Sandra is a master with them. Listen to her.

Q: Can I use AI in my writing samples or submissions.

Sandra:
For the most part, editors want your manuscript to contain current, research-based information. They also expect your manuscript to be composed of your original writing. The path you take to get there, is pretty much left up to you. In general, you should NOT use AI as a cited source, yet it may be suitable for gaining a basic understanding of a topic or for other precursory purposes. AI is unreliable and prone to errors. The advice from one of my publishers was to use it with *caution and skepticism.* Bottom line, use AI *extreme* cautiously unless your publisher's guidelines state specific policies about its use.

Mike:
AI is a slowly opening Pandora's box that's currently causing a free-for-all in publishing markets. It will take a while before commonly accepted standards are put in place. My suggestion is do *not* use AI unless it is clearly stated you are allowed to do so. My most recent contracts state that the use of AI is prohibited.

www.ingramcontent.com/pod-product-compliance
Lightning Source LLC
Chambersburg PA
CBHW081153270326

41930CB00014B/3134